The
TAO
of
TRADING

Also from Dearborn by Robert Koppel
Praise for *Bulls, Bears, and Millionaires*

"*Bulls, Bears, and Millionaires* doesn't just attempt to demystify the world of trading, it explores the souls of those who reside in it. It's insightful, honest, and entertaining—a fascinating read for both veteran traders and interested observers of the markets."

—William J. Brodsky, Chairman and CEO
Chicago Board Options Exchange

"You feel as if you are eavesdropping on compelling tales, not about trading, but about the vastly diverse roots and incredible forces that drive these people so."

—Stephen Franklin
Chicago Tribune

"*Bulls, Bears, and Millionaires* brings the trading world to life like never before. Bob Koppel's interviews reveal the stories of some of the world's top traders, many of whom overcame considerable odds before achieving their success. I highly recommend this book."

—John F. (Jack) Sandner, Chairman
Chicago Mercantile Exchange

"Bob Koppel's knowledge of trading and gift for writing allow him to reveal the mind and essence of some of the outstanding traders of our generation."

—Solomon Cohen, CEO
CK Partners

"*Bulls, Bears, and Millionaires* gives the reader a rare glimpse into the world of the professional trader. Written by one who has 'been there, done that,' Bob Koppel uncovers the much overlooked factors that ultimately determine success or failure in the high stakes arena of trading. Must reading for anyone who thinks successful speculation results from simply studying charts and watching *Wall Street Week . . .*"

—Scott A. Foster, President
Dominion Capital Management, Inc.

The
TAO
of
TRADING

Discovering a Simpler Path to Success

Robert Koppel

Dearborn
Financial Publishing, Inc.®

Editorial Director: Cynthia A. Zigmund
Managing Editor: Jack Kiburz
Interior Design: Lucy Jenkins
Cover Design: Scott Rattray, Rattray Design
Illustrations: Mara Koppel
Typesetting: Eliot House Productions

Published by Dearborn Financial Publishing, Inc.®

Printed in the United States of America

98 99 00 10 9 8 7 6 5 4 3 2 1

Library of Congress Cataloging-in-Publication Data
Koppel, Robert.
    The Tao of trading: discovering a simpler path to success / Robert Koppel.
        p.   cm.
    Includes bibliographical references and index.
    ISBN 0-7931-2598-7 (hard)
    1. Futures. 2. Taoism. I. Title.
    HG6024.A3K666   1998   97-42762
    332.64'5—dc21   CIP

Dearborn books are available at special quantity discounts to use as premiums and sales promotions, or for use in corporate training programs. For more information, please call the Special Sales Manager at 800-621-9621, ext. 4384, or write to Dearborn Financial Publishing, Inc., 155 N. Wacker Drive, Chicago, IL 60606-1719.

DEDICATION

To my family
Mara, Lily, and Niko

"Everything should be made as simple as possible,
but not simpler."

—*Albert Einstein*

CONTENTS

FOREWORD

Desire, hard work, and hustle had always been the formula for success in the typically Western, left-brain-dominated world that I grew up in. This formula had worked throughout my life in sports, school, and relationships, and I fully expected it to ensure success in a trading career. Of course, it did help me gain some very useful experience and professional recognition.

Through years of covering and executing for the retail options market, quants and technicians, and for the largest, most powerful institutional investors, I learned enough about fear and greed to eventually start speculating on my own. In retrospect, I realize that I had the perfect background to become a "successful" but inconsistent trader: emotional and obsessed with the bottom line.

A short while ago, I began to explore a completely new and different body of knowledge to gain insights into how to take my trading to the next level. I was drawn to a wide array of works about psychology and optimal performance. After reading Bob Koppel's earlier works (*The Innergame of Trading, The Outer Game of Trading,* and *The Intuitive Trader*) as well as some other books he recommended, I had my great awakening.

It became so intensely obvious that I already had all the empirical and intellectual skills required to be truly successful, and that we all possess unlimited potential. Most importantly, I became aware of some ancient principles that helped to align me with the natural flow and energy of the events in my life. Every day now, thanks to this new attitude, I work on developing my focus, intuition, confidence, assertiveness, detachment, egolessness, and integrity. Cultivating my personal attitudes has become just as important and real to my trading as the hard work and hustle of doing the fundamental, technical, and quantitative analyses.

In truth, I am still not fully present in every moment, or even most moments, but with the knowledge and framework that Bob Koppel has masterfully pulled together in *The Tao of Trading*, I have periods where I see things more clearly and have become aware of the many courses of action that lead me to almost effortless yet extraordinary performance. Getting to that centered assertive zone has become the goal; the bottom line merely follows. As you read *The Tao of Trading*, you will realize that the concepts that Bob writes about are not new but are used by many of the most successful people in all activities in life.

It is as a result of Bob Koppel's profound and diverse knowledge of philosophy and psychology tied with his frontline, trading experience that has made these concepts so understandable and user-friendly. I am grateful that Bob has synthesized these concepts in a coherent text. Read on and I think you will find that in *The Tao of Trading* your journey will truly become your reward!

—Tom Grossman
President, SAC International Equities, LLC.

PREFACE

"The truth knocks on the door and you say,
'Go away. I'm looking for the truth.'
And so it goes away."

—Robert M. Pirsig, *Zen and the Art of Motorcycle Maintenance*

The undeniable, singular essence of successful trading is this: *welcoming truth knocking at your door.* It is our choice to be mere spectators or to become players fully engaged in the action. For those who have learned to recognize the sight, sound, and feel of its knock, trading becomes a game, a journey, a dance, and an astonishing personal odyssey of self-realization. However, for those others who haven't, trading becomes a menace, a frustration, a painful activity of repeated negative associations and fear-driven experiences.

The difficulty for the writer is in devising a way to transform trading from a noun to a verb—how to write about it in a way that does not convey a mere intellectual or emotional description and how to bridge the gap between second-hand conceptual theories and first-hand experiences that don't fit conveniently into any rigid system of pigeonholes or ideas.

I think there is much to be learned in this regard from the writings of the East. As I pointed out in *The Intuitive Trader*, in the West there is a strong rational-empirical bias against concepts of "unarticulated truth," truth that is arrived at through nonrational (i.e., nonlinear, metaphorical, imaginative) forms. However, embracing these concepts brings us much closer to a complete understanding of the trader's psyche. The important point here is that the experience of successful trading at its essence is subjective, unself-conscious, and intuitive. This state of mind has more in common with the spirit of jazz—improvisational, automatic, and responsive to the riff—than with a well-articulated and analyzed process of decision making.

In *Zen and the Way of the Sword: Arming the Samurai Psyche*, Winston L. King writes, "The warrior no matter how well trained in the techniques of his martial skills had to break through the superficial layers of his ordinary reasoning, his habit-ridden mentality, to the deeper center of his true original self."

Samurai training was founded on its unique understanding of the human mind and what might be called the mind's "inner truth reality." The samurai was involved in a disciplined process of deepening and expanding his awareness until it permeated the total self and governed every thought and action. Truth was existential and experiential, not intellectual.

Survival for the trader is just as real! Every trader knows that market truth is existential, not intellectual; its realization and practice are visceral, not cerebral. Market wisdom, like samurai truth, is practiced truth that can only be utilized and realized in action. It can never reside on the level of mere theory.

It has been my goal in *The Tao of Trading* to create a text that is written in a style to speak to the reader's imagination and "nonrational" side through metaphor, stories, interviews, autobiography, and epigram, much in the same way as do Phil Jackson's *Sacred Hoops* and Eugen Herrigel's *Zen in the Art of Archery*. I believe I demonstrated in *The Intuitive Trader* that trading at the highest levels of achievement, as with all expressions of peak performance, is being in possession of the ability and freedom to act according to one's own inward perception and feelings of reality apart from the conventional wisdom, rules, and techniques of "sound" trading practices.

The Tao of Trading therefore does not seek to explain or describe market truths but rather to indicate and open doors. The reader is invited to see the markets and trading as they really are—alive, dynamic, robust, and not to be dissected and analyzed like a corpse lying on a slab. I think Alan Watts's comment about his book *The Spirit of Zen* sums up this idea well: "A proper exposition of Zen should tease us out of thought. It should leave the mind more like an open window than a panel of stained glass."

I wish you success in trading (and everything clse)!

ACKNOWLEDGMENTS

I wish to thank the many traders who generously shared their ideas and insights into the workings of their creative minds; in particular, I would like once more to recognize my friend and business partner, Howard Abell, for his inestimable contributions. I would also like to thank Mara Koppel for reading the original manuscript and for providing her fine suggestions, all of which were taken. Thanks also goes to Cindy Zigmund and the staff at Dearborn Financial Publishing for their uncompromising support throughout this project.

Finally, I would like to thank my many readers, who once again make all my work worthwhile.

THE TAO AND TAOISM

According to Chinese tradition, the Tao (pronounced *dow*) originated with Lao-Tzu, who was born in 604 BC. He is an enigmatic figure who is frequently pictured as being a solitary recluse, down-to-earth, a genial man with a ferocious sense of humor and joyousness. His name itself, Lao-Tzu, can be translated as "old boy," "old fellow," or "the grand old master." He never preached or organized any religion and did not seek fortune or fame.

According to Huston Smith, author of *The World's Religions*, Lao-Tzu, saddened by people's disinclination to cultivate the natural goodness with which he believed they were endowed, sought personal solitude. As legend has it, he climbed on a water buffalo and rode westward to what is present-day Tibet. At the Hankao Pass, a gatekeeper tried to persuade this strange-looking itinerant to turn back. Failing this, he asked Lao-Tzu to leave a record of his beliefs for the civilization he was abandoning. Lao-Tzu retired for three days and returned with a slim volume of 5,000 characters titled *Tao Te Ching (The Way and Its Power)*. It is a testament to humanity's sense of itself in the universe; it can be read in half an hour or over a lifetime and remains to this day the basic text of Taoist thought.

The Tao teaches that each of us possesses limitless power and potential that we can realize when we align ourselves with the natural flow of energy and events. The Tao promotes personal growth and improvement and advises us to respond to life's challenges like water yielding, by not forcing unnatural energies, and by following the natural path of least resistance.

According to the *Tao Te Ching*, pursuing the Tao brings one in tune with the way of the universe, the rhythm and harmony of all things: "The more it is drawn upon, the more it flows, for it is the fountain ever on. It is graceful instead of abrupt, flowing rather than hesitant, infinitely generous and powerful."

"The great Tao extends everywhere.
All things depend on it for growth,
And it does not deny them . . .
It clothes and cultivates all things,
And it does not act as master . . .
In the end it does not seek greatness,
And in that way the great is achieved."

—Lao-Tzu, *Tao Te Ching*

PART ONE

The Artist's Mind

The Spirit of Jazz

Walk into any art museum or gallery and it is immediately apparent that artists perceive and process life differently than most of us. The artist's mind blazes new trails and makes unexpected stops on a creative map that takes it to original destinations. The unique aspect of the artist's mind is its subtle ability to insinuate truth: to demonstrate truth not by describing someone else's version of it but by pointing through metaphor and symbol to the magical, ever-elusive spirit, rhythm and atmosphere of truth that is at the same time novel and accessible.

I say *magical* in the sense that it generates energy to both artist and recipient as it stimulates and invigorates thought, vision, and meaning. Magical in a way logic can never be. In portraying the art of Picasso, Norman Mailer in his book *Picasso* explains that whatever provides us with continually enhanced connotations is magically endowed.

A ceremony, a person, or an object is able to enrich us only when its nature, its "artful" nature, rewards further study or calls for more relationships. That is to say, its nature transcends familiarity. And that indeed may be why good poetry is more magical than good prose—the message is more elusive, more compressed, and more responsive to sensuous study.

The choreographer Agnes de Mille said, "Living is a form of not being sure, not knowing what next or how. The moment you know how, you begin to die a little. The artist never entirely knows. We guess, we may be wrong, but we take leap after leap in the dark."

Understanding the essential nature of the artist's mind provides, I believe, an exciting and richer interpretation of the creative and intuitive depth of the world's greatest traders. In writing about trading, two extremes constantly need to be avoided: One is defining and explaining so little that the reader is completely bewildered, and the other is describing so much that the reader is convinced that he or she truly understands all!

In my experience and association with top traders, I have come to the conclusion that great trading is, in fact, an aesthetic rather than an analytical experience. It is an activity better characterized by right-brain words such as *imaginative, subjective, artistic, intuitive, metaphorical,* and *feeling,* rather than left-brain words such as *analytical, objective, scientific, logical,* and *rational.*

Of course, it would be grievously incorrect to underestimate or deny the importance of logic, science, and reason in the trading process. However, successful trading as practiced by the world's top traders involves far more than merely calling upon specific analytical or strategic skills. It requires the development, cultivation, and conditioning of habits, thought patterns, and creative attitudes that influence the way to think and behave in the market.

Turn to almost any book that has ever been written on the subject of trading, and you will find some or all of these trading axioms:

- Buy low, sell high.
- The trend is your friend.
- Avoid the crowd.

- Take small losses.
- Take big profits.
- Don't overtrade.
- Manage your money well.
- Don't turn a profit into a loss.
- Don't add to a losing trade.
- Don't get stubborn.
- The market is always right.
- Buy the rumor, sell the fact.
- Trade liquid markets.
- Don't buy or sell on price alone.
- Preserve capital.

Unfortunately, knowing all the rules or mastering a particular objective trading system is about as far removed from the experience of optimum trading as painting by numbers is from producing a Picasso. In *Sacred Hoops*, Phil Jackson writes:

> When I was named head coach of the Chicago Bulls in 1989, my dream was not just to win championships, but to do it in a way that wove together my two greatest passions: basketball and spiritual exploration.... In basketball—as in life—true joy comes from being fully present in each and every moment, not just when things are going your way. Of course, it's no accident that things are more likely to go your way when you stop worrying about whether you're going to win or lose and focus your full attention on what's happening right now.... For me, basketball is an expression of life, a single, sometimes glittering thread, that reflects the whole. Like life, basketball is messy and unpredictable. It has its way with you, no matter how hard you try to control it. The trick is to experience each moment with a clear mind and open heart. When you do that, the game—and life—will take care of itself.

There is something intangible, subjective, and intuitive about trading that involves a state of mind that has more in common with the spirit of jazz—improvisational, automatic, and alive—than with an objective rule-based system of rational decision making.

Personally, jazz has been one of my great loves from the time I was small. If I close my eyes and look inward I can immediately hear the music of Bud Powell, Bill Strayhorn, Eric Dolpky, Clifford Brown, Miles Davis, and McCoy Tyner on command. Like great trading, jazz is a lot easier to recognize than to describe. I am reminded of Fats Waller's curt reply to a critic who once asked him to define jazz. "If you don't know it by now," said Fats, "don't mess with it!"

Jazz, like all great music, makes certain technical demands and requires a strong discipline of the player. In that respect, it is no different from playing the Beethoven Quartets or Bach's Goldberg Variations; however, there is something unique and, I believe, helpful to traders about listening to the music of Charlie Parker, Duke Ellington, and John Coltrane or intensely following a lyric sung by Ella Fitzgerald, Carmen McCrae, or Shirley Horn. Of course, it is not to say one ought to prefer Ellington to Beethoven or that Coltrane or Parker are more worthy of exploration than Bach. That of course would be ludicrous!

There is something, however, about the essence and spirit of jazz that, for me, presents itself as a perfect metaphor for understanding trading. At its core, jazz has always been obsessed with experimentation—whether it is the early music of Louis Armstrong or the later music of Coleman Hawkins. As with trading, one can "feel" the psychological demands on each artist playing his or her instrument imperfectly poised on the edge of chaos. It is a psychological landscape that is violently alive with altering and blurred snakes and hairpin turns. A universe without regular and Euclidean shapes. It is at the same time straight, curved, jagged, gnarled, twisting, sedentary, and dashing—always spontaneous and rarely predictable.

Jazz is an art of improvisation. Individual style, tone, ideas, and structure express the player's personality; whether it is the introspective, convoluted, intense, and fretful music of Miles Davis or the rollicking, madcap, joyous style of Fats Waller or the unique bebop sound of Thelonius Monk. The point is that spontaneous creation is the lifeblood of the music itself.

In his book, *Jazz Is,* Nat Hentoff records one musician's assessment of what it takes to be a successful player. It is a description to which most traders will immediately resonate.

> It's like going out there naked every night. Any one of us can screw the whole thing up because we're out there improvising. The classical guys have their scores, but we have to be creating, or trying to, anticipating each other, taking chances every goddamn second. That's why when jazz musicians are really putting out, it's an exhausting experience. It can be exhilarating too, but there's always that touch of fear, that feeling of being on a very high wire without a net.

The ancient Chinese saying that "The journey is the reward" is as true for the trader as it is for the jazz musician. The journey is at one and the same time exploding with possibility however fraught with risk—to leap or not to leap into the dark. The challenge for both is to find his or her own unique way beyond fashionable or "common-sense" assumptions that have no compelling relevance for the individual. It is on the far side of philosophical absolutes, beyond the clinging comfort and psychological security of firm principles, on the very edge of chaos that we need to discover our own voices as traders, musicians, and human beings. It is learning to feel at home in what Zen refers to as "the great void ..., above, not a tile to cover the head; below, not an inch of ground for the foot."

At first glance, such a view as it relates to music or trading may seen somewhat exotic. The point I'm trying to make is that there is something about trading, like art, that is mysterious, contradictory, irrational, and inscrutable—what the Taoist would call beyond conventional understanding, beyond what we can represent to ourselves or others in words or other formal systems of notation. Consider the following passages from the *Tao Te Ching*: "There was something vague before heaven and earth arose. How calm! How void! It stands alone, unchanging, it acts everywhere, untiring. It may be considered the mother of everything under heaven. I do not know its name, but call it by the word Tao."

"The Tao is something blurred and indistinct.
How indistinct! How blurred!
Yet within it are images.
How blurred! How indistinct!
Yet within it are things.
How dim! How confused!
Yet within it is mental power.
Because this power is most true,
within it there is confidence."

"The Tao's principle is spontaneity."

"The great Tao flows everywhere,
to the left and to the right.
All things depend upon it to exist, and it
     does not abandon them.
To its accomplishments it lays no claim.
It loves and nourishes all things,
but does not lord it over them."

"When the superior man hears of the Tao,
he does his best to practice it.
When the middling man hears of the Tao,
he sometimes keeps it, and sometimes loses it.
When the inferior man hears of the Tao,

he will laugh aloud at it.
If he did not laugh, it would not be the Tao."

"Those who know do not speak.
Those who speak do not know."

—Lao-Tzu, *Tao Te Ching*

In *Hear Me Talkin' to Ya* (Shapiro and Hentoff, 1966), Charlie Parker says "Music is your own experience, your thoughts, your wisdom. If you don't live it, it won't come out of your horn." It is remarkable how similar is this statement to Bryan Gindoff's answer when I asked him in *Bulls, Bears, and Millionaires* what distinguished him from all other traders: (Gindoff is a screenwriter and portfolio manager.)

I guess I would also ask myself what makes me a different writer from all the other writers out there? The answer is I have my own voice. It's something that I've learned to project and identify as truly my own. A voice is a very subjective thing. It's your individual style or way of telling a story that you have developed over time as a result of a lot of soul searching and hard work. I think as a trader, the same thing applies. If you've been able to create a voice as a trader, that's your individual approach and method of identifying opportunity. Whether a writer or a trader, your voice is what is uniquely you.

Picasso said that painting cannot be taught, only found. The great traders, like all artists, are moved by an internal Tao, an inner voice in tune with its own rhythm and harmonies, improvising wildly while growing a talent based on an open mind and heart's willingness to receive the market and the world. Swiss psychologist Carl Jung stated a similar notion this way: "The creation of something new is not accomplished by the intellect but by the play instinct acting from inner necessity. The creative mind plays with the object it loves."

Am I suggesting that the world's best traders are engaged in a form of artful play? Indeed I am! Moreover, I would propose, based on my own experience and interviews with hundreds of top traders, that the "spirit" of their trading is what is truly unique and in the end successful for them. Is it any wonder that someone can read scores of texts on trading techniques and strategy and not experience the trading performance of a George Soros? Personally, I would love to buy a couple of books on the opera and immediately after completing the last volume, break into song like Pavarotti. Unfortunately, it is not to be!

Listen, in their own words, what the top traders have to say. Consider their words not as philosophy but rather as the Tao saying prescribes, "An old pine tree preaches wisdom, and a wild bird cries out truth." Personally I think the choice of the word *spirit* is very apt in describing the uniqueness of each trader. Originally I considered the word *truth* (i.e., market truth); however, I later rejected it because I felt the idea of truth seemed too enshrined. Spirit conveys more of the vitality and sense of aliveness—the dynamic nature of traders and markets. Many of us have experienced more than once that, as soon as we felt we had grasped ultimate market truths, the truth soon vanished. Truth cannot become anyone's property, because it is chaotically alive and evolving. In *The Spirit of Zen*, Alan Watts writes, "...truth is life, and for one person to think that he possesses all life is a manifest absurdity. The part cannot possess the whole."

The *Chuang-Tzu*, which, besides *Tao Te Ching* is the other great Taoist text, tells the following story:

> Shun asked Ch'eng, saying, "Can one get Tao so as to have it for one's own?"
>
> "Your very body," replied Ch'eng, " is not your own, how should Tao be?"

"If my body, " said Shun, "is not my own, pray whose is it?"

"It is the delegated image of Tao," replied Ch'eng. "Your life is not your own. It is the delegated harmony of Tao.

Your individuality is not your own. It is the delegated adaptability of Tao.

"You move, but know not how. You are at rest, but know not why…. These are the operations of the laws of Tao. How then should you get Tao so as to have it as your own?"

As soon as one tries to possess truth, an attempt is made to define it. The Taoist would say the idea of possession is illusory. Life (i.e., trading) can never be grasped it must be lived. As Alan Watts explains in *The Way of Zen,*

Accepting the Tao means not running away from life but running with it, for freedom comes through complete acceptance of reality. Those who wish to keep their illusions do not move at all; those who fear them run backwards into greater illusions, while those who conquer them "walk on."

"When they curiously question thee, seeking
  to know what it is,
do not affirm anything, and do not deny
  anything.
For whatsoever is affirmed is not true,
and whatsoever is denied is not true.
How shall anyone say truly what that may be
while he has not himself fully won to what is?
And, after he has won, what word is to be
  sent from a region
where the chariot of speech finds no track
  on which to go?

> Therefore, to their questionings offer them
> silence only,
> Silence—and a finger pointing the way."

> —*Tao Te Ching*, as quoted by Alan Watts

The Top Traders

Scott A. Foster

Mr. Foster is president and CEO of Dominion Capital Management, Inc., a trading firm that specializes in global financial derivatives with $200 million under management. Before forming DCM in 1994, Mr. Foster was senior trader for AO Management Corp.

It has been obvious to me from the beginning that I'm dealing with the best and the brightest in the world. I believe that the smartest people in the world are not curing cancer; they are in the financial markets, because that's where the money is. And that if I am going to make a dollar, I have to pry a dollar out of somebody else's hands. And when you begin to look at it that way, that's when you understand that there are two sides to the marketplace. If you want to buy a contract, somebody's got to sell to you, and if he's going to sell it to you, he equally and oppositely believes what you believe or he wouldn't be doing it! When you begin to look at the marketplace in that light, you need to be certain about what is your edge. You have to do what makes you think you can compete effectively with these traders and institutions, trading firms that have a whole host of

Ph.D.s and professional traders who have been there for years, with unlimited financial resources and research capabilities.

I was never under the illusion that I could outreach some of these firms when it came to understanding some of the fundamentals. For me, it was more a matter of concentrating on market tone, market psychology, and the more temporal aspects of trading. The key is that you must know what your edge is and respect the competition because it is fierce: talented, hard working, and well-capitalized!

The market teaches you to expect the unexpected and be prepared for it! You end up in situations that you don't think you're ever going to end up in, where you're forced to make decisions. You can't delay. You don't have time to think about it. The market's trading, and you've got to get out of a position or you have to do something. You also find yourself in situations that you don't want to be in despite all the preparation. So you must be quick-thinking and nimble. You have to learn to understand and manage the leverage. You've always got just enough leverage to hang yourself, and nobody's there to stop you! What I have learned is that through trial and error and several near-death experiences, I have survived and am very good at what I do.

I know also that I've been able to come back from 70, 80 percent drawdowns, and then have gone on to make new equity highs. I have never not made a new equity high. And I've gone from day trading to spread trading to doing a variety of different strategies and styles in many different marketplaces. I think I'm very good at exploiting psychology. I really feel that I could go to any market that trades in the world and make money. You must know your edge at all times! I've talked to traders who have hit a losing streak and they can't figure out why they're not making money. I always ask them, "What were you doing when you were winning?" and sometimes they don't know what they were doing or why they were winning. They aren't able to identify what they bring to the market that is unique and allows them to exploit opportunity.

If you asked, what does Scott Foster bring to the market that's unique, I'd say I feel it's more my psychological approach to the marketplace rather than any particular methodology. I gravitate toward identifying what works. I've gone for periods where I only traded the cattle market. I've gone for stretches where I've done nothing but trade spreads. I've gone for months where I only day-traded the S&Ps. Fortunately, all of those experiences have been positive. You must be flexible and versatile. You can't bet on knowledge of just one market or one technical or tactical approach. If you do, you find that suddenly the market changes and you are like a deer caught in the headlights.

"What is true of archery and swordsmanship also applies to all the other arts. Thus, mastery in ink-painting is only attained when the hand, exercising perfect control over technique, executes what hovers before the mind's eye at the same moment when the mind begins to form it, without there being a hair's breadth between. Painting them becomes spontaneous calligraphy. Here again the painter's instructions might be: Spend ten years observing bamboos, become a bamboo yourself, then forget everything and—paint."

—Eugen Herrigel,
Zen in the Art of Archery

Jack Sandner

Mr. Sandner, formerly a trial attorney, joined the Chicago Mercantile Exchange in 1971 and has served continuously on its governing board since 1977. He is currently chairman of the board.

He is president and CEO of RB&H, Inc., a futures commission merchant.

I think you'd have to go back to the recesses of the mind, what makes someone competitive, and what makes someone want to win. You learn that the desire to win and the ability to try to figure a way to win in whatever venue you're involved complement one another. For example, if it's boxing, the desire to win may translate into training very, very hard, working on different skill sets rather than just going in and being a brawler. You'll find a way to win, and usually it's through hard work and discipline....

In boxing, if you're fighting a certain kind of a fighter, you'll fight a little differently. Is he a strong puncher or a stick-and-move-type of fighter? I'm always trying to find a way to score the points to win or to get the knockout. But the main thing is to walk out the winner at the end! I think everybody prepares for trading differently. In my case, I think because of my competitive nature, I saw the markets as just another event....

I think I just always had the intuitive feeling that winning was a protracted experience in trading and not a one-time thing. Once you can adjust to that and truly understand it's the whole game that counts, then you can look at the market in an objective way.

It isn't a daily thing, because nobody can be a daily winner. You develop rules and discipline and an approach. Of course, you also have to know that to win you must create a set of standards and movements. And it takes time to do that through trial and error! But the key is to respond as a winner to what happens to you in the market. If the fear of losing is so extraordinary that it inhibits you from moving forward, you cannot be a trader. Also, you cannot be an all-or-nothing trader. You can't trade with the attitude that I'm going to make a million today or I'm going to lose everything I have. That's a disaster! I say you must view trading as a protracted experience and then know how you respond as an individual. I find that people who turn out to be terrible traders are the ones who don't know how to respond to what they would define as a loss. They just don't know how to react. Their fear of losing keeps them in the market too long! It puts them in positions that they wouldn't otherwise have been in. Ultimately you need to have a healthy respect for the market, and the fear of losing cannot be so pervasive in your system that it doesn't allow you to trade to win. You can watch children as they are growing up. You can tell which kid plays not to lose and which one plays all-out to win. There's also the kid who won't dive off the board because he's just too afraid! Or the opposite, the kid who is reckless and gets hurt. To be a successful trader, you need to understand the balance point between being too afraid and too aggressive.

"Give all your nights to the study of Talmud and your days to shooting from the hip."

—Irving Layton, Poet

Mike Dever

Mr. Dever is president and CEO of Brandywine Asset Management, a Commodity Trading Advisor managing $200 million.

I constantly like new challenges, learning new things. I would get incredibly bored if I went home and watched TV every night. So the main attraction of trading for me is that it's always new. There's nothing that's the same one day to the next. I've talked to people who were always trying to find out what they wanted to do in life. With me, it was a matter of how many lives I could fit into just this one! I've always had so many things I wanted to do. I've been fortunate that

I've had a fascination with trading from a young age, and became addicted enough early on to have spent the last 18 years focused on building that interest into a successful business.

I've heard people talk about a particular trader and say how, you know, he was a natural, a born trader—that the person had an intuitive sense of the markets. But frankly, I think intuition without experience is really just good luck. Some people do start trading and immediately make money. Others will say that they were born to trade. From my viewpoint they were lucky. Intuition is not innate. It is simply the instinctual processing of accumulated knowledge. It grows from experience, and that's what really forms the basis of consistently successful trading.

"The best advice I've ever received is the advice I have for young broadcasters: The best way to sound like you know what you're talking about is to know what you're talking about. But young broadcasters rarely ask for advice. How did you get your job? How much money do you make?—That's what they want to know."

—Scott Simon, National Public Radio

Solomon Cohen

Mr. Cohen runs CK Partners, Inc., in New York City, investment advisers to the Gazelle Global Fund Limited. The Gazelle Fund was the top-performing equities fund in 1995. He worked at James Capel & Co. in derivative sales and proprietary trading before leaving to start his own firm.

Trading has taught me different things about myself at different times according to how the situation has gone. It has taught me that I can be very disciplined, that I don't have to have external constraints imposed on me. It's taught me that I'm very self-reliant. Often I can put together the jigsaw puzzle, even though some pieces are missing and will have an insight into a trade that other traders don't perceive. Sometimes I realize I've been arrogant in the way I've done something.

It's interesting how trading teaches us something about ourselves that we don't necessarily want to know but the information is always very instructive.

I am always thinking about my trading. I look back, and analyze how things have gone: Why I took certain decisions. What I did with information that was available to me. How I have interacted with other people in the marketplace. And it's always a learning experience.

For me, trading is something which is completely natural and instinctive. It's not something that I really think about. When I get into discussions with brokers or dealers about the way they want to handle a deal I can see some clear differences between us.

If I had to generalize it, I would say that I think diagrammatically, in terms of abstract structure. Others tend to be more focused on detail, on smaller perspectives. Sometimes I feel like I'm looking at the whole room, while others are squinting through a keyhole.

This orientation comes from my background in math and music, because both mathematics and music are about structure and about the ability to see structures. If you think about algebra and how we arrive at general solutions to problems, it can be widely applied to a whole range of things. So we're looking for patterns and symmetry, and from there you can work down and apply concepts to individual situations and the music is also about structure.

Often people don't see the structure in music. I mean just recently my father was saying, listening to something that Beethoven composed, "God, this is so wonderful. I don't know how somebody could have created this!" In fact, the music represents a combination of the creative, something raw and original, with a pattern and structure, a method to develop the idea musically.

Without this structure, the music would appear without form. It would not be a sonata or a symphony. It would merely be chaotic!

> "If one really wishes to be master of an art, technical knowledge of it is not enough. One has to transcend technique so that the act becomes an 'artless art' growing out of the unconscious."
>
> —D.T. Suzuki, *Zen Buddhism*

Timothy McAuliffe

Mr. McAuliffe is a member of the International Monetary Market. He has been a member and floor trader at the Chicago Mercantile Exchange since 1982.

I'm not afraid to fail. Take basketball for example: I definitely can miss a last shot, but it's not because I choked or was indecisive. I want the ball in my hand. I don't want it resting in somebody else's. But you have to have discipline too. I think if there is one common trait among all successful traders it is discipline. So although I might want to take the last shot, I'm not going to throw up a brick and if I've gone zero-for-ten that day, I'm going to call a time out to make sure the best possible shot gets taken. I never forget the object of the game is to take home the victory!

My father was an All-American football player, and he expected, no, demanded, excellence. He never was the typical parent. He didn't say things like, "My son is the greatest," or "My son can't do anything wrong." In today's society, it's always encourage, encourage, encourage! My father took almost the opposite approach. He expected that we would have successes and therefore when we did, even when we received the adulation of the local town or our peers or whatever, he always came down hard on us. He didn't want us to think that this was the end of the road or that our pot of gold was winning the town championship! He made it very clear that there were other goals to achieve. There were other levels to attain and he always emphasized that you can't rest on your laurels. Excellence is a life long standard!

Trading has taught me a lot about the frailty of the individual. How in the blink of an eye you can be blown out of here! When you experience something like Black Monday with that type of volatility, you realize how nuts this whole thing is. You could get trapped in a position, and be wiped out before you know what hit you. That's why I said before trading is all about adaptation. If you don't adapt immediately to a situation like that, you're history. And that's why, as a trader, there's no ironclad set rules to follow because in order to be successful you have to change not only to the market but to a variety of situations that are constantly in flux.

It has also taught me something else that I really got from my father but it has been reaffirmed in the market. You need to have discipline and a strong sense of your own moral code, a sense of honor, if you will. This may sound a little overblown, but you also need the personal honesty to not be afraid of the truth.

If I had cancer and was dying, I wouldn't want anybody protecting me from that fact. I wouldn't want someone trying to ease my pain. Just tell me! If you can't handle the truth, that's OK, but I've got to deal with the truth every day of my life and I can't have it whitewashed. What I've learned is that, no matter, what I can handle the truth and I think that gives me a huge advantage in the market.

Larry Rosenberg

Mr. Rosenberg is a long-term member of the Chicago Mercantile Exchange and is a past chairman of its Board of Directors. He is president of Lake Shore Asset Management and PMB, a Futures Commission Merchant.

My father was a scrap dealer, which was really a way of playing markets, in a much riskier way than I do. He was doing it with real inventory. He had an inventory that he would either sell or be stuck with! So risk-taking is in my background on many different levels.

I started by scalping corn and rye. Back in those days, you very rarely had a one-cent range during the entire day, trading eighths. I was doing a lot of spreading in odd lots. It was a tough grind. I had to do other things to supplement my living. I sold clothes three evenings a week and on Saturdays. I clerked at the exchange in the afternoons. I did whatever had to be done so that I could trade and pay my expenses.

I think the guys who have been around for a long time from my generation—that's almost a defining quality of their personalities. They do whatever it takes to succeed in trading and everything else. The successful traders over the years are survivors—you have to be. And you do whatever it takes to survive and sometimes it means getting "real creative."

I think it's the mark of a survivor. The ones who are not tough fall by the wayside. Look down at the bar after the market closes: the ones who won't make it are drinking their brains out!

I've always been pretty good about the emotional side. I never really took it out on anyone in my family. I might not have been real happy, but I never blamed anyone else. You know, it's not the market's fault. It's not the computer's fault. It's not the clearinghouse's fault. It's your fault when you screw up. And ultimately to be successful you must know that. Not read it in a book but live it day in and day out every day you trade.

"If you want to please the critics, don't play too loud, too soft, too fast, too slow."

—Arturo Toscanini, to Vladimir Horowitz

Toby Crabel

Mr. Crabel is a long-term trader and market analyst. He has been a floor trader and wrote a newsletter that market professionals closely followed. He is currently a Commodity Trading Advisor, managing over $100 million.

It is a long and difficult process. There were times when I would make more money than I thought at all possible, when the dollars just sort of fell in my lap. And then there were times when I couldn't even sleep at night because I was just so excited. When I lost money, I was just terribly depressed. It had a huge effect on me. So the emotion really was affecting me whether I made or lost!

Early in 1987 I had a four-month drawdown that really set me back. I questioned whether I even wanted to trade at that point. I took a year to reevaluate the whole thing. That's when I wrote my book, *Day Trading with Short-Term Price Patterns and Opening Range Breakout*. It was a great time for personal reflection.

I realized that what I loved about trading is the intellectual challenge of the business. And I decided that I could never leave. I wanted to be involved in it and I knew it was something I could do. So I regrouped, came back to Chicago, and started writing a market letter that I sold to floor traders. Then in 1990, I ran into another drawdown. And that was it for me! The moment of truth. In 1987, I was committed to figuring out what it would take to create a proper program to run a business as a professional trader. The thing that I learned very clearly in 1990 was that the volatility had to drop dramatically so that I could control the risk. By 1992, I had all the mechanisms in place. Unfortunately, it wasn't quite as systematic as today. But the thinking process was there.

In reality, the answer was completely moving away from discretionary trading to the point where I am today. I am completely systematic in my approach. It was hard to give up the discretion!

Actually it took me until early 1995 to finally become comfortable with something and that I thought was better than what I could do on a discretionary basis. It was developing the systematic approach which allowed me to eliminate the volatility: the emotional volatility and the uneven trading performance.

"It is not the same to talk of bulls as to be in the bullring."

—Spanish proverb

Marshall Stein

Mr. Stein is senior vice president of Rand Financial Services and a member of the board of directors, Chicago Mercantile Exchange. He is an independent trader and former member of the Chicago Board of Trade.

Trading has certainly taught me about my personal strengths and weaknesses. It has taught me how I react under situations of stress.

Trading has allowed me to have a measure of courage in what I do for a living. It has shown me that I have the capability to rise to an occasion to exhibit, if you will, grace under fire.

It's not like I go around pounding my chest, but it's a comforting thought to know that I have the courage to trade markets at times when it feels like I should run scared. I can exercise strength of character to either stick with it or get out.

It's the analysis sometimes, or the work that you've done. It's the culmination of your thinking that you've put into action.

I think what distinguishes me from most is that I have really done just about everything that is possible in our profession and I am still on the lookout for new challenges.

"One of the most significant features we notice in the practice of archery, and in fact of all the arts as they are studied in Japan and probably also in other Far Eastern countries, is that they are not intended for utilitarian purposes only or for purely aesthetic enjoyments, but are meant to train the mind; indeed, to bring it into contact with the ultimate reality. Archery is, therefore, not practiced solely for hitting the target; the swordsman does not wield the sword, just for the sake of outdoing his opponent; the dancer does not dance just to perform certain rhythmical movements of the body. The mind has first to be attuned to the unconscious."

—Eugen Herrigel,
Zen in the Art of Archery

Robin Mesch

Ms. Mesch is the chief fixed-income technical analyst for Thomson Research, one of the largest providers of proprietary

financial information services in the world. Robin authors
Trading Prophets—CBT Bonds, *a fixed-income market newslet-*
ter providing trading strategies and analysis on the 30-year
Treasury bond.

There's a phase that you go through where you think you can't
lose. And you teach yourself you just know exactly what the market is
going to do next. Then to compound problems, you think, since I
can't lose I might as well pyramid as the market is going against me.
That's how strong you feel about that. But you need those experiences
of being wrong so you can learn to become a disciplined trader, which
in the final analysis is ultimate control. You learn from your mistakes
if you're committed to paying attention.

"The new mass of knowledge is still form-
less, incomplete, lacking the essential
threads of connection, displaying misleading
signals at every turn, riddled with blind
alleys. There are fascinating ideas all over the
place, irresistible experiments beyond num-
bering, all sorts of new ways into the maze of
problems. But every next move is unpredictable, every outcome uncertain.... I do not
know how you lay out orderly plans for this
kind of activity, but I suppose you could find
out by looking through the disorderly
records of the past hundred years. Somehow,
the atmosphere has to be set so that a dis-
quieting sense of being wrong is the normal
attitude of the investigators. It has to be
taken for granted that the only way in is by
riding the unencumbered human imagination, with the special vigor required for recognizing that something can be highly

improbable maybe almost impossible, and at the same time true."

—Lewis Thomas, *The Lives of a Cell*

Tom Shanks

Mr. Shanks is president and CEO of Hawksbill Capital Management, a Commodity Trading Advisor. He is a former "Turtle." The Turtles were a group of handpicked traders who were mentored by Richard Dennis.

I think that anybody who goes through a drawdown questions whether what he's doing is correct and whether the systems are still viable, so there's a real struggle with that. For me, experiencing a drawdown is a tremendous motivation to get back on track. There's a reassurance when you get back to analyzing things and realize that drawdowns happen. You tell yourself that ultimately you will come out of it. It's obviously very hard on the client and your own state of mind, but it's part of the whole process. You've got to take care of yourself on a personal level, make sure you're getting enough rest and exercise and that kind of thing. Make sure you're bringing enough energy to the effort. So there's a lot of personal management involved as well.

You can't kid yourself in trading. You have to deal with who you really are, and take responsibility for all your shortcomings, which the markets have a way of revealing rather starkly. You have to confront all your fears and tame them. You have to check your ego at the door.

You learn from each experience. There's nothing in life that you can do that can guarantee that you're not going to go through some pain. Trading is certainly not a singular pursuit in that regard. What

I have learned is this: Patience and diligence are rewarded. Profits will eventually accrue if you do the right thing and stick with it. That's the most important thing!

Arlene Busch

Ms. Busch heads one of the world's most successful proprietary trading groups for Refco, Inc. Previously, she served as director of trading and risk worldwide for Cresvale International Management. She traded as a local for nine years at the Chicago Board Options Exchange.

One of the things that I pride myself on is not having an ego about this business. Having a big ego about trading is a recipe for disaster. It's what will make a trader lose every penny he's made. If I find a trader in the group who has a big ego, I immediately let them go. I don't care how much money they're making. You can tell by watching how they're trading. They'll get stubborn about a position. They'll think that they're right and the market is wrong! The market is never wrong; the market is always right!

But you can see their ego in other things as well. You see it in their habits and possessions. They drive Ferraris. They wear gold Rolexes! They live in outlandish houses. They fly the Concorde. I don't want traders who do this. I want traders who respect the market and keep their personal egos in check.

Bryan Gindoff

Mr. Gindoff is a screenwriter residing in Los Angeles, California. Previously, he was president of Del Rey Investment Management.

On Wall Street, just like in Hollywood, you want to look for a very strong story that's so powerful that it can succeed in spite of what might not be great execution, and if you can find great execution to go along with it, then you really hit the jackpot. For instance, in the last five years, one of the strongest stories has been computer networking stocks. About five years ago if you looked at the world and said, "Hey, there are all these zillions of computers out there and somehow they're all going to have to get tied together so they can communicate with each other," well, you had an incredibly strong story there.

So then if you went looking in the networking sector for stocks to buy, as opposed to other sectors of the market, you dramatically increased your probability of making a much higher return on your money. There's a good chance that you could have done quite well for a while just buying a large basket of networking stocks because the market was recognizing the strength of the basic idea and carrying poor to average companies along for the ride with the very good companies. You see that all the time in the market.

And if you went the next step and identified the leaders—Cisco, Cabletron, 3Com, for instance, then you really did make tons of money. Essentially those were the companies that not only had the compelling story idea, but they also executed it with great dialogue and a great cast.

I think there really is a good analogy between how you make money in the movie business and how you make money in the market. Movie studios make their big money from blockbusters, which are often referred to as "tent-poles," the pictures that hold up the tent, so to speak. Generally, if you're going to have a shot at making outsized returns in a portfolio, you need a few tent-pole stocks— core holdings where you concentrate more of your money because you've found a company or a few companies with compelling stories, and, hopefully, great execution too. In both arenas I believe the biggest money is almost always made when you can tap into the compelling themes....

I think trading has taught me a lot about myself. As a matter of fact, I think the whole process, if you allow yourself to really be open, is like going through psychotherapy everyday. It really gives you an opportunity to see what you're all about.

The market forces you, if you're going to succeed, to be completely honest with yourself. If you're losing money, you are simply forced to confront that reality. It's an objective reality, it's right in front of you, and you have to acknowledge it. Truthfully, I believe the market weeds out people who are unable to be honest with themselves. I suspect that trading, aside from being a fascinating way to make a living, is also one of the most self-revelatory things that a person can do. Day in and day out you're confronted with all your primal emotions.

"I merely took the energy it takes to pout and wrote some blues."

—Duke Ellington

Tom Grossman

Mr. Grossman is president of SAC International Equities, LLC. He was formerly the head foreign equities trading strategist for Kingdon Capital Management.

In high school I played football and lacrosse and I was also a swimmer. In college, I concentrated exclusively on football. I certainly think the competitive element, the discipline involved in succeeding at sports, spills over to most occupations, but trading particularly....

Early in my career at Kingdon, the Japanese equity market was extremely weak. The Nikkei had broken 15,000 and everyone in the world was bearish. I started to feel on a purely intuitive basis and then later on a more dogmatic or quantitative basis that the market was ready to take off and I built a case for a long position in what was a very illiquid, difficult market to trade. The result, however, was that I picked the bottom of the market and had an extremely profitable trade! And I think that defines my confidence in my own intuition and investment process. You must have the courage of your own convictions to buck the trend and act on your own intuitive beliefs....

I find you have to recognize when you have an advantage. If you're not sitting with a position in a market that's getting killed, that's a tremendous advantage because you don't have the emotional pain that everyone else is experiencing. It's almost your duty or responsibility to yourself to play. I say to myself, there are traders in pain here, losing their cars and houses, whatever, and it's time to play. I have to take action. You can smell the blood of other people's losses. That has to kick up on your radar screen, you must seize that advantage. In fact, that's what makes the game worth playing....

I actively search for opportunities that no one else is looking for. And I have the confidence to do the trades, to try them and to know that I'll be wrong a lot. And I have the conviction that overall I'm still going to come out way ahead.

What happens to me a lot of times is I do a great deal of work on a theory or strategy and the actual trade comes down to no value. And unless you derive that pure joy of identifying and getting the edge when it is there for a minute, a day, a week, or a month, then you won't be able to tolerate all the dead ends. As long as that joy is with me I've got to be confident that I'm going to stay at the head of the pack. I know and have seen fertile areas of opportunity come and go because information has become more widely accessible. My edge is to constantly stay out in front of the curve. I'm not afraid to identify it and then take my shot!

> "You've got to be very careful if you don't know where you are going, because you might not get there."
>
> —Yogi Berra

Angelo Reynolds

Mr. Reynolds is a member of the International Monetary Market, where he trades his own account. He specializes in the Eurodollar contract.

I learned a long time ago in sports there is a world of difference between thinking and doing. I was afraid and I think it was a natural fear. I mean I was going against some of the best traders in the world! But in no way did I ever believe that I wasn't going to succeed like I had in everything else I ever did in my life.

The first trade I made I bought ten contracts. The market immediately went in my direction and I made $250. It was an exhilarating feeling!

I was really feeling good and didn't see a lot to do in the market until later in the session. And there it was! I saw something that I thought could really pay off and was committed to play to win. So I stepped out and bought 100 contracts and I was right again! At the end of the day I had made $5,000. I got home and my wife greeted me at the door. All I said was, "Honey, we're going to be rich."

It was one of the best feelings I have ever experienced in my life. I felt I was put to the test and proved my mettle. You really never know how people are going to perform in high-pressure situations until they're placed under fire. I have seen guys on the trading floor with degrees from Harvard not make it and others right off the street who've proved themselves brilliantly. Some guys just get in the pit and freeze up. Other guys can't tolerate the uncertainty....

There was one trader in particular who could be very intimidating. I told him, "Look, you might scare the rest of these guys, but you don't scare me!" This guy was supposed to be something, like a fifth-degree something or other in martial arts and everybody was afraid of him. When he would come in the pit he would shadowbox to show people that he had karate skills and could fight. He just had a reputation of being a tough guy and, on top of that, he was a very big trader. So people were just naturally intimidated by him. He would trade 500 or 1,000 at a clip and treated the other locals shamelessly and none of them would ever say anything to him. About a month after I arrived in the pit, I bought 300 contracts from one of the brokers at a time when this trader was heavily short. Apparently he didn't like that and he started calling me all kind of names. I just let him know right then and there that he could talk all he wanted but he wasn't going to intimidate me. I said to him, "Hey, there is just air between me and you, if you want to do something, I'm right here, have a piece of me." I'm from West Philadelphia. Believe me, there were a lot of tough guys where I came from!

I think that fear is something that everybody deals with, even the greatest athletes. I was watching an interview with Mike Tyson. He was talking about a fight that he had when he was a teenager. Before the fight he was petrified. He was scared shitless! But once he got in the ring he wound up knocking out his opponent in 17 seconds! His manager told him something that I have found to be true and very useful. It is very simple: Everybody's afraid. It's what you do with that fear that separates the guy who is a coward from the guy who is courageous. Personally, I would rather give it my best shot and fail than to look back and say I didn't have the courage to really "be there" in trading and everything else.

"Honesty is the best policy and spinach is the best vegetable."

—Popeye

"You see things vacationing on a motorcycle in a way that is completely different from any other. In a car you're always in a compartment, and because you're used to it you don't realize that through that car window everything you see is just more TV. You're a passive observer and it is all moving by you boringly in a frame. On a cycle the frame is gone. You're completely in contact with it all. You're in the scene, not just watching it anymore, and the sense of presence is overwhelming....the whole experience is never removed from immediate consciousness."

—Robert M. Pirsig,
Zen and the Art of Motorcycle Maintenance

The top traders perform on motorcycles of their own making as active agents, where their sense of presence is nothing less than overwhelming. They trade in the here and now, focused on each new moment like jazz musicians meeting on and off an improvised beat. One is like Dizzy Gillespie: outgoing, gregarious, and at the same time reflective and lyrical. Another plays in the clear piano style of

John Lewis, intellectual and immaculate. Still another delivers the breathtaking tempos of Art Tatum. Each is successful for they are moved by his or her own creative spirit, characterized by originality, authenticity, and unflinching honesty. For them the Tao of trading is vital and alive.

It is a continuously fresh musical progression, like hair blowing in the wind—its texture and line splashed with life, always there, strange, mysterious, seductive, and unknown.

PART TWO

Samurai Psyche

The Sword of Mastery

"The samurai warrior tended to scorn the life of the courtier as soft and lacking vigor, roughness, directness and above all 'action' was demanded of him. The bushi lived a rigidly disciplined life."

—John Hall,
Japan: From Prehistory to Modern Times

There is a striking similarity between the discipline needed in the trading theater and on the battle lines between the feudal lords of ancient Japan. In the midst of the fray, there was no time for the samurai to think about the proper way to launch an attack or swing a sword; technique needed to be second nature so that the warrior could concentrate on "proving" victorious. When it came time to act, if the knowledge to do so was not integral to the warrior or there was even the slightest degree of hesitation, his battle was over. Likewise, the traders effective action needs to be reflexive, disciplined, and prerehearsed.

Consider this description of the samurai swordsman (Suzuki, *Zen and Japanese Culture*):

> The perfect swordsman takes no cognizance of the enemy's personality, no more than of this own. For he is an indifferent onlooker of the fatal drama of life and death in which he himself is the most active participant. In spite of all the concern he has or ought to have, he is above himself, he transcends the dualistic comprehension of the situation, yet he is not a contemplative mystic, he is in the thickest of the deadly combat.

D.T. Suzuki makes a similar point by humorously comparing the fight to the death with a slightly more mundane activity.

> The swordsman is not to make a show of bravery, nor is he to feel timid. He will also hardly be conscious of the presence of an enemy, or in fact of himself as confronting anybody. He will act as if he were conducting his everyday business—for instance enjoying breakfast. Let the swordsman handle his sword as if he were handling chopsticks picking up a piece of food and putting it into his mouth.

Of course, consuming one's opponent is not an alien idea to traders. Traders often speak of the way trades taste in a colorful linguistic range from that runs from bitter to sweet, also, when things are not going well we routinely get "eaten up" by the market. One of the most common expressions used on the floors of the Chicago exchanges to explain the importance of taking small losses and allowing profits to run is, "You can't eat like a bird and shit like an elephant!" I've also heard traders refer to trading choppy markets as trying to "chew" on razor blades. But to return to my original point, the samurai operated in a very physical and dangerous context. Their sense of truth as it related to the perfection of their arts, was life-surviving. Their discipline was simple, spare and natural. Their lives were spartan, based not on the truth of doctrine, culture, or rarefied learning, but on the unself-conscious, nonintellectual, creative, responsive warrior mind of action.

In my judgment, the toughest part of trading is learning how to overcome the rigid intellectual guardianship's of the left brain, which serves to habituate existing behaviors and to rationalize the need for logical consistency—and emancipate the intuitive right side of the brain, the key to changing ingrained thought patterns and habits.

Characteristics of the Right and Left Hemispheres of the Brain

Left Hemisphere	Right Hemisphere
Analytic	Imaginative
Objective	Subjective
Deductive	Inductive
Timebound	Timeless
Scientific	Artistic
Conscious	Unconscious
Logical	Intuitive
Rational	Feeling
Intellectual	Metaphorical
Verbal	Internal
Realistic	

The right brain serves as a clearinghouse for our intuitive and creative mental functions. As traders, the difficulty for most of us is that often we receive an intuition or imaginative impulse, these "flashes" from the beyond are immediately dispatched to the left side of the brain for interpretation, selection, and analysis. We know the actual portion of the brain that performs this function. It is called the *corpus callosum*.

It must be remembered, of course, that the left brain performs an invaluable service for us. Without it, we could not function effectively as human beings, because of all the information that comes into our perceptual field from moment to moment. It is indispensable in determining, at any given moment in time, what is important for us to know. In *Your Maximum Mind*, Herbert Benson sums up the dilemma well:

> ...unfortunately, the left side of the brain is so important in its function that it has tended to overshadow the role of the right side of the brain. Yet the right side is the key to the plasticity of our minds, to our ability to change ingrained thought patterns and habits.... the left side of the brain, with its powerful abilities to analyze and make convincing influences, may be portrayed as a kind of "little dictator" over the right side. Many of our intuitive and creative functions, as well as much information that we need to know and use in changing our lives for the better, have in effect been enslaved by our rational left hemisphere. You might say we have become prisoner of the left side of our brains.

Traders need to be able to respond to information quickly and accurately from within in order to take effective action in the market. For many of us, changing existing trading habits, thought patterns, and attitudes remains the most significant challenge. And it is not enough just to know this! What is required is nothing less than an internal revolution of awareness that leads effortlessly to the adoption of unself-conscious action. As Benson puts it, "we must overthrow the hegemony of the left hemisphere and allow the right to break free and assume its full stature in the thinking process. In this way we can hope to open the door to beneficial change and growth in our lives."

For the trader, as for the samurai, second-guessing and analysis at the decisive moment where only action is called for destroys split-second timing and spells defeat. Action free of thoughts, reflection, memories, or any other internal hindrance is the key to a successful result, whether it is victory in battle or accumulating trading profits. The unconscious must be allowed to occupy the entire field of perception (e.g., intuition, imagination) so that what is primarily there is a force of instinctual irresistibility making free use of the consciously accumulated knowledge. This is what is known as Yagyu's sword of Mystery (Suzuki, *Zen and Japanese Culture*).

> However well a man may be trained in the art, the swordsman can never be the master of his technical knowledge unless all his psychic hindrances are removed and he can keep his mind in the state of emptiness, even purged of whatever technique he has obtained. The entire body together with the four limbs will then be capable of displaying for the first time and to its full extent all the art acquired by the training of several years. They will move as if automatically, with no conscious effort on the part of the swordsman himself. His activities will be a perfect model of swordplay. All the training is there but the mind is utterly unconscious of it.

It must not be assumed that what Suzuki is referring to is some blind celebration of visceral feelings, a philosophy of trust your gut to the extreme. The samurai depended on a "highly educated gut." However, it was one that came from a profound existential understanding of the role of the unconscious. The Yagyu school of swordmanship taught you were only a master of the art when the technique worked through your body and limbs as if totally independent of your conscious mind. Suzuki described it as follows:

> When actions are directly related to the problem of life and death, they must be given up so that they will not interfere with the fluidity of mentation and the lightning rapidity of action. The man must turn himself into a puppet in the hands of the unconscious. The unconscious and instinctive

must supersede the conscious. (Suzuki, *Zen and Japanese Culture*).

Let's consider for a moment how the samurai's art is similar to the jazz musician's art. At first, the samurai practices his movements and strokes repeatedly more accurately, incessantly, until his technique is ingrained into his nervous system. He is, so to speak, "hardwired" through manual practice, discipline, and preparation. The jazz musician too must work the score until the music becomes part of him or her. Through memorization and repeated play, the musician develops intellectual and emotional mastery of the music so that he or she "feels" its every nuance in the nerves and muscles. Both are engaged in a process that follows a course that begins with conscious awareness of specific physical and intellectual skills and leads inevitably to an unconscious moment of truth when notes and fingers play, and mind and muscle are one: a perfect, inexpressible blending of mental powers of perception and focus with the physical powers of execution.

"The Tao that can be told of
is not the absolute Tao;
The names that can be given
are not absolute names."

—Lin Yutang, *The Widow of Lao Tse*

This passage is from the *Chuang-Tzu*:

"There is great beauty in the silent universe. There are manifest laws governing the four seasons without words. The sage looks back to the beauty of the universe and penetrates into the intrinsic principle of things. Therefore the perfect man does nothing, the great sage takes no action. The spirit of the universe is subtle and informs all life. Things live and die and change their forms without knowing the root from which they come. Abundantly it multiplies; eternally it stands by itself."

—Winston L. King,
Zen and the Way of the Sword

"We take a handful of sand from the endless landscape of awareness around us and call that handful of sand the world. Once we have the handful of sand, the world of which we are conscious, a process of discrimination goes to work on it. This is the knife. We divide the sand into parts. This and that. Here and there. Black and white. Now and then. The discrimination is the division of the conscious universe into parts... no two are alike.... Shades of color in different piles—sizes in different piles—grain shapes in different piles—subtypes of grain shapes in different piles—grades of opacity in different piles—and so on, and on, and on. You'd think the process of subdivision and classification would come to an end somewhere, but it doesn't. It just goes on and on."

—Robert M. Pirsig,
Zen and the Art of Motorcycle Maintenance

For the trader, as for the samurai warrior and jazz musician, being fully engaged requires the seemless unity of emotion, intellect, and physical technique beyond all divisions into a harmonious living flow: swordsmen and sword, musician and music, trader and market.

> "No think, no reflecting
> perfect emptiness:
> Yet therin something moves,
> following its own course.
> Victory is for the one,
> even before the combat,
> who has no thought of himself,
> abiding in the no-mind-ness of great origin."
>
> —Lao-Tzu, *Tao Te Ching*

Before us is a most interesting and challenging question: How is the trader to overcome ordinary reasoning, habit-driven behaviors, and self-defeating attitudes, and emancipate the right hemisphere of his or her brain to execute learned trading techniques in a visceral, unconscious, and intuitive way? In other words, how is the trader to perfectly blend creative awareness with the mechanical skills of trading?

The simple, strong, and strict discipline of the samurai warrior provides a solid foundation on which to build a trading philosophy, allowing also for a certain amount of poetic license and a jazz musician's need for improvisation, I would offer the following: Learn the shared characteristics and attitudes of all the top traders and then simply ask yourself whether you believe you possess these same qualities and beliefs. Do you see yourself as a top trader?

The Personal Characteristics of Top Traders

Confident	Hardworking
Disciplined	High-achieving
Self-reliant	Energetic
Motivated	Objective
Competent	Proactive
Self-aware	Organized
Optimistic	Goal-oriented
Intuitive	Self-contained
Honest	Knowledgeable
Strategic	Open-minded
Patient	Determined
Enjoy trading	Ambitious
Risk-managing	Committed
Focused	Manage stress
Independent	Automatic
Risk-taking	

[handwritten: Success cycling — pos, neg and neutral minds]

[handwritten: Risilient Victorious]

The Shared Attitudes of Top Traders

- They understand their motives for trading.
- They develop trading strategies that work for them because they fit their personalities.
- They enjoy trading and make it effortless.
- They work hard at developing their skills and maintaining a trading edge.
- They trade with total confidence in themselves and their methodology.
- They trade in a positive state of mind that allows them the flexibility to act automatically and know exactly the next right step to take in the market.

The Shared Attitudes of Top Traders, continued

- They intuitively understand money management and risk-control and know that no single trade is worth everything.
- They have a strategy that works and the discipline to carry it out.
- They are independent-minded and understand that they are personally responsible for all market decisions.
- They understand the difference between loss and losing.
- They understand the importance of acting at difficult times with circumscribed risk.
- They know what drives markets and the difference between hope and fear.
- They don't trade to please others.

It is important to be able to visualize yourself possessing these qualities and attitudes in a literal sense. The reason is that trading requires an incredible amount of effort, commitment, and discipline. If this shoe does not feel right, it is going to be hard to march forth! The French writer Antoine de Saint-Exupéry observed, "That which is essential is invisible to the eye." This is particularly true in trading, where subjective belief and internal discipline are the main determinants of success or failure. In *Leo Melamed on the Market*, Melamed writes:

> The type of person you are—the way you react under pressure, your ability to make quick decisions, to think logically, the strength of your character, the emotional quotient of your personality, your philosophical approach towards money will determine your probable chances of success or failure in trading. In trading, more so than perhaps in any other field of endeavor, your psychological makeup is critical. Alas, such characteristics are generally hidden from view. Baseball Hall-of-Famer Honus Wagner said it all when

he remarked, "There ain't much to being a ball player if you're a ball player!"

Life and Death Requirements for Every Trader

I. Learn a Proven Trading Methodology

Learn a methodology that is personal, profitable, and consistent and then remember Einstein's words of advice: "Everything should be made as simple as possible, but not simpler." The purpose of keeping it simple is simple: so you can act!

II. Learn How to Take a Loss

Knowing how to take a loss for the trader is as significant for him or her as learning to overcome the fear of death was for the samurai warrior. In *Zen in the Art of Archery,* Eugen Herrigel recounts the following tale as told in the Hagakure, which dates back to the middle of the 17th century:

> Yagyu Tajima-no-kami was a great swordsman and teacher in the art to the Shogun of the time, Tokugawa Iyemitsu. One of the personal guards of the Shogun one day came to Takima-no-kami wishing to be trained in fencing. The master said, "As I observe, you seem to be a master of fencing yourself; pray tell me to what school you belong, before we enter into the relationship of teacher and pupil."
>
> The guardsman said, "I am ashamed to confess that I have never learned the art."

"Are you going to fool me? I am teacher to the honorable Shogun himself, and I know my judging eye never fails."

"I am sorry to defy your honor, but I really know nothing."

This resolute denial on the part of the visitor make the swordmaster think for a while, and he finally said, "If you say so, it must be so; but still I am sure you are a master of something though I so not know of what."

"If you insist, I will tell you. There is one thing of which I can say I am a complete master. When I was still a boy, the thought came upon me that as a samurai, I ought in no circumstances to be afraid of death, and I have grappled with the problem of death now for some years, and finally the problem of death ceased to worry me. May this be at what you hint?"

"Exactly!" exclaimed Tajima-no-kami. "That is what I mean. I am glad that I made no mistake in my judgment. For the ultimate secrets of swordsmanship also lie in being released from the thought of death. I have trained ever so many hundreds of my pupils along this line, but so far none of them really deserve the certificate for swordsmanship. You need no technical training, you are already a master."

For the samurai, conquering his fear of death was more than a simple declaration of warrior readiness. It was, in fact, central to his understanding of reality itself. In *Zen and Japanese Culture*, Suzuki writes:

Those who cling to life die, and those who defy life live. The essential thing is the mind. Look into this mind and firmly take hold of it, and you will understand that there is something in you which is above birth and death and which is neither drowned in water nor burned by fire.... Those who are reluctant to give up their lives and embrace death are not true warriors.

Conquering his fears of death was the samurai's testament that one can transcend the limits of intellectuality that create all the dualities that impose a restricted view of life: good-bad, inner-outer, man-world, and life-death. Winston L. King in *Zen and the Way of the Sword* suggests this attitude was a kind of Japanese "Invictus":

> The Zen meditation discipline served to strengthen the firmness of that inner platform of mental control on which he [the samurai] sought to stand in time of combat by making it impervious to the shakings of any and all distractions—purely incidental factors, the desire for victory, hunger for fame and fortune, and most especially the fear of death.

In "Bushido: Mode or Ethic?", Roger T. Ames states:

> The resolution to die and the strength and intensity of this commitment is constantly reinforced through meditation, making it the focal point of the bushido existence. It is the center of the bushi mentality from the moment of decision until the moment of consummation. It is a resolve which must be total and immediate, and which can only be achieved by contemplation on and affirmation of this single principle. In short, death becomes the essential meaning of life.

For the trader, the essential issue that needs to be resolved once a viable trading approach has been mastered is overcoming the fear of loss. To state the problem succinctly, the question for the trader is whether it is possible to be psychologically divorced from the long-term goal of profitability from the immediate and short-term trauma of incurring losses.

In the movie *Wall Street,* Gordon Gekko states the dilemma aptly: "Nothing ruins my day like losses." The most common ways traders handle the issue of loss are the following:

Denial. Is it any wonder that most traders are not getting the results that they want in the market? I think not! The reason I have come to this conclusion is that most traders choose to trade with their eyes closed, ears shut, and nervous system turned off. How else could you tolerate a trade that continues to go against you, day after day, with no defined risk, until the discomfit has gotten so severe that even the psychological Novocain you've self-administered can no longer stave off the pain? Denial won't help. In the words of Loretta Casterini to Ronny Camerarri in the movie *Moonstruck,* "Snap out of it!"

Inaction. As the old saying goes, "if you sleep on the floor, you can't fall out of bed." Unfortunately, many traders have adapted this position when it comes to the question of risk. If you don't pull the trigger, they "feel," you can't miss the target. But the truth of the matter is that you have to pick up the gun and steady your aim—that is, know what you're shooting at—before you can pull the trigger with confidence. Developing a trading approach with a specific point of focus and possessing the psychological understanding that taking a loss (the real fear) is not only inevitable but essential will give you the conviction to exploit market opportunities and not miss out.

It is only when missing out becomes more painful than being inactive that triggers get pulled and targets get hit!

Confusion. Confusion and uncertainty result from not working out a well-defined risk management formula prior to entering a trade. You will recognize that reevaluating the cost of your family's vacation while your position is sinking to new lows is not an optimum trading strategy. The more emotion that can be eliminated from your trading, the greater your sense of clarity about market decisions. Jeffrey Silverman made this point very well when interviewed for *The Innergame of Trading*: "Doing things that avoid having an emotional content in your decision-making is where all the discipline comes in…. Be unemotional about getting in, be unemotional about the position, and be unemotional when getting out."

Anger. Reacting to the market out of anger is like choosing to hold your breath until your neighbor turns blue. It's not going to work! Your anger will not affect the loss positively. It certainly may influence it negatively by turning a small loss into a large one!

The Truth about Taking a Loss

Why is it that in the many hundreds of books that I have read on trading and investment, the word *loss* rarely rears its ugly head? Its omission is like a collective denial of an Ebola-like virus, ignored in the mistaken hope that, if it is not acknowledged, it will quietly leave without taking victims. The truth is loss for the trader is the perfect analogue for what death is for the warrior. It is omnipresent and real. Stated quite simply, learning to take a loss is the single hardest and most important lesson that a trader has to learn. This is no intellectual lesson; taking a loss involves every aspect of the human being. The following describes how traders typically respond to taking a loss.

Physical symptoms of taking a loss:
- Rapid or shallow breathing
- Sweating
- Constriction of muscles
- Upset stomach
- Tension
- Feeling of malaise

Emotional symptoms of taking a loss:

- Angry
- Depressed
- Disillusioned
- Distracted
- Generalized anxiety
- Irritable
- Frustrated
- Low self-worth
- Embarrassed

Visual imagery traders see when taking a loss:

- Sights of past failures
- Pictures of trading obstacles and disappointments
- Visions of unrelated mishaps of a generalized nature

Auditory imagery traders hear when taking a loss:

- The voice of doom and failure
- Recordings of negative experiences from the past
- Memories explaining why he or she is such a "jerk"

Sensory imagery traders feel when taking a loss:

- Body feels heavy
- Shoulders drop
- Torso is hunched
- Facial muscles slacken
- Breathing is short
- Eyes are cast down
- Trader feels slow, weak, or out of energy

Anxiety traders experience when taking a loss:

- Fear of failure—trader feels intense pressure to perform and ties self-worth to trading

- Fear of success—trader loses control; euphoric trading; trader doubts himself
- Fear of inadequacy—trader experiences loss of self-esteem, diminished confidence
- Loss of control—trader loses sense of personal responsibility when trading; feels market is out to get him

Thoughts traders have when taking a loss:
- "I don't know what I'm doing."
- "These markets are impossible."
- "I'm too small, inexperienced, young, old, etc."
- "I don't have a clear strategy."
- "What will X think of me?"
- "I'm a loser, fool, idiot, etc."

Beliefs traders possess about themselves and the market when taking a loss:
About the market—

- "The market is rigged."
- "It's impossible to have a winning trade."
- "The locals always pick me off."
- "You can never get a decent fill."
- "My broker's out to get me."

About themselves—

- "I can never make a winning trade."
- "I'm such a _____. I always make the same mistake."
- "I have to be perfect."
- "If I take a loss, then I'm a loser."
- "If the market doesn't do exactly what I expect, I don't know anything."

Self-defeating attitudes traders possess when taking a loss:
- Holding yourself to impossible standards
- Trying to please others
- Thinking in absolute terms—black or white, all or nothing, total success or failure
- Focusing on negative things
- Believing your childhood or past experience have programmed you for failure.
- Demanding certainty of yourself and the market
- Defining trading as impossible
- Representing a bad trade as a catastrophe
- Labeling yourself a globally negative way rather than just looking at the trade.

As you read over each of these characteristics, ask yourself the following questions:

- How does all this relate to me?
- How do I personally experience taking a loss?
- What physical symptoms do I experience?
- What emotions do I have when taking a loss?
- What do I hear in my mind's ear?
- What sensory imagery do I experience?
- What specific anxieties do I have of a recurring kind?
- What am I thinking when I take a loss?
- What do I believe about myself and the market when taking a loss?
- What self-defeating attitudes do I possess when taking a loss?

If you answer each of these questions with the samurai's commitment to truth, to overcome life's greatest fear, you certainly will have positioned yourself well to better understand the essential nature of trading.

The Top Traders

The following interviews reveal the samurai psyche as practiced by top-performing traders.

Joseph Siegel

> *Mr. Siegel was a long-time member and market maker on the floor of the Chicago Mercantile Exchange.*

All successful trading comes down to three things: knowledge, nerve, and the ability to lose money.

Everybody has the ability to lose money, but it takes nerve to lose and then choose to stay in the game—to want to come back, to have the audacity to assume that you're smart enough and quick enough to make your trade and take advantage of opportunities and make money. I found that the psychology of being able to lose money and come back was a big factor, because it's very easy to lose money and very easy to become discouraged. You have to have a great deal of confidence in yourself that even though you've taken a beating in the market, whatever form it takes, you can come back, you can return and trade effectively.

Donald Stevens

> *Mr. Stevens is a long-time member and independent trader at the Chicago Mercantile Exchange.*

You must define certain parameters. Frequently when I enter a market I can't see the market going too much against me or I'm out.

You must have a strict code that you can apply with discipline. You must act consistently and decisively.

Gene Agatstein

Mr. Agatstein is a long-time member of the International Monetary Market and a former floor trader specializing in the currency market.

Successful trading gets right down to the psychology of self-esteem and self-confidence. If you're trading long enough and intensely enough, I think ultimately the statistics have to work in your favor if you just hold on to the winners and cut the losers. So why doesn't it work for everyone? The answer is self-confidence.

I also think it's kind of hard to disentangle money management from this whole issue of self-esteem and self-confidence. If you're thinking dollars and cents on each trade, whether you're right or wrong, the amount of money can be very intimidating. I think everybody overtrades a little bit, overreaches when they feel good. They get a little bit too committed to a position. If you're unlucky enough to get hit, you could be out of business. But for me, in order to make money, I believe you have to be willing to risk your trading capital. If I'm in the market and am adequately capitalized, I'll sit down with a pencil and paper and figure out how much I can lose on this trade, where I think the trade can go against me and how much that would translate into dollar losses. I think my strongest and best performances have been when I've in fact lost money on a trade initially and have been tested to that point—when the market's turned around and left me in my trade. I always feel they can't hurt me anymore. They hurt me and I survived and now I'm riding the right way with the market. It's that sort of snapping back, that sense of being down money and then finding yourself back in the game.

George Segal

Mr. Segal is an independent trader and long-term member of the Chicago Mercantile Exchange. He is the former president and CEO of CSA, Inc., a Futures Commission Merchant.

I think that successful traders have a personality, that they're not afraid to have 19 losing trades out of 20, because the twentieth can be a trade that's much greater than the other 19 put together. They're not hung up on losing money. They want to protect what they've got and wait for the opportunity to make a lot of money.

They're willing to accept the loss, to take a loss and come back and make another trade, and know there's always tomorrow. There's always another trade to be made tomorrow. They don't like to take a big loss.

The only thing I think about when I make a trade, I'm never thinking about how much I'm going to make. I'm always concerned about where I'm going to get out if I'm wrong.

Money management is probably the most important thing, I would say, whether it's $100,000 or $10 million. What holds most traders back is not being able to admit they're wrong. I think a lot of people have trouble admitting they've made a mistake, that this is not the right time. The timing was off, or the market's not ready. Maybe there are other factors in this market you don't know about. They're just not willing to admit that they're wrong.

There are also people who are afraid to go into trades, but they shouldn't be trading if they're afraid to get involved, even if it's only a one lot. I mean I would assume a lot of people have gotten out of trading because they're afraid to make trades.

Another thing: Everybody can get out of a winning trade. It's pretty easy to get out of a winning trade—most people get out of a winning trade much too soon. But it's very hard to get out of a losing trade. When I'm in a trade, I'm looking to see how far the market can go and where I think it can go. I'm looking to maximize. I do have a target when I go into it and I try not to pay too much attention to the market while it's going good. I don't like watching every tick. Many times the best markets I've ever had were markets that I've added to the positions, bull positions on strength and bear positions on weakness. Because I feel convinced now that the market has corroborated my thinking, that it's now going to do what I thought it would do.

Bruce Johnson

Mr. Johnson is an independent trader and market maker in the Chicago Mercantile Exchange livestock markets. He is president of Packers Trading Co.

You know, I've looked at all of the people that I know and they come from such diverse backgrounds. You watch somebody like Joel Greenberg and you watch somebody like George Segal, Lloyd Arnold, and Bob Rufenacht. I always thought that the only common thread that ever ran through all of these people was that they all kind of had a gross disregard for money. Look at Bob Rufenacht. I worked for him for several years and watched him go up and down several times. The money never bothered him. It never bothered him to lose it. Everybody says, "If I made a million dollars I'd quit." That mentality will never make a million dollars. I think the real players really and truly don't focus on the money.

Jeffrey Silverman

Mr. Silverman is an independent trader and long-term member of the Chicago Mercantile Exchange, where he serves on its board of directors.

I look at what I think the risk is in a position. I look at what I think the return is likely to be. I try and maximize what's in my account in terms of the most bang for the buck, in terms of return for risk, in terms of return for margin dollar investment. Then, as I've gotten more successful, I tend to just keep dialing down the amount of risk per margin dollar so that I can trade with an even longer-term perspective.

Leo Melamed

Mr. Melamed is chairman emeritus of the Chicago Mercantile Exchange and is an active futures trader and chairman and CEO of Sakura-Dellsher Investment Company, Inc., a Futures Commission Merchant.

You have to get the emotions out of the way. You have to strip yourself from emotions and you have to intellectualize. The emotions should not be anywhere near your decision-making process. Emotional reactions are the worst reasons to make a trade or make a decision. That was my strongest asset; an ability to remove personal emotion from a market decision. Whenever I let emotion dictate, I had to clean the slate, get out of the market, step away from the trade, and regain my equilibrium.

III. Learn the Psychological Skills of Winning

Based on interviews that I have conducted with hundreds of top traders as well as my own experience as one of the leading market makers on the Chicago Mercantile Exchange trading floor for over a decade, I have compiled the following list of specific psychological skills that are critical for success in trading:

- Compelling motivation
- Goal-setting
- Confidence
- Focus
- State management
- Positive imagery
- Mental conditioning

The Syntax of Successful Trading

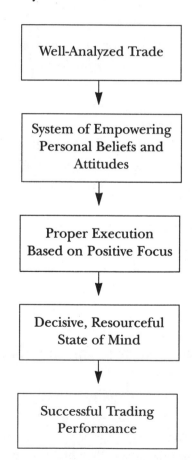

Compelling motivation. Compelling motivation is possessing the intensity to do whatever it takes to win at trading—to overcome a bad day or setback in order to achieve your trading goals. Think of the intensity of a world-class athlete: fully engaged and not afraid to play the game, not afraid of "being there," totally involved in the moment.

Goal-setting. Goal-setting is imperative to the trader not only in terms of setting realistic and measurable goals within the context of a specific time frame, but also in terms of enhancing motivation and performance. It in fact conditions the trader on an ongoing basis to boost his trading to the next level. It is excellence, not perfection, that is the point here—excellence produces results; perfection produces ulcers.

Confidence. Confidence based on competence is purely a result of motivation, belief (in oneself and the market) and state of mind. Confidence in psychological terms is no more than consistently expecting a positive outcome. Think of anything you have ever done in your life with that feeling of confidence (positive expectation). Did not that feeling ultimately predict a successful result? It is the same with trading.

Focus. The tighter your focus and the finer the distinctions you bring to your trading focus, the better the results. Focus is one of those terms that sound like a cliché unless you understand how to utilize it in your trading. It is through focus that one stays consistent and is able to maintain a high level of confidence. Focus derives from developing a specific strategy that allows you to feel certain and act accordingly.

State management. How you feel at any given moment will determine your state of mind, including what you feel physically, represent visually, and process emotionally about your trading.

Learning how to manage your state of mind will determine whether you hesitate or act and whether you are emotionally drained or physically and psychologically energized.

Successful Trading Performance

Bodily Response	**Visualization**	**Auditory**
Body feels light, shoulders are erect; torso is straight. Facial muscles are taut; breathing is deep and relaxed.	Seeing yourself succeed. Watching yourself in control, relaxed. Looking competent, confident and positive. Eyes looking up and straight ahead. Trader is feeling strong, energized and enthusiastic.	The voice of confidence and control. The sound of relaxed, effortless trading.

The Winning State of Mind

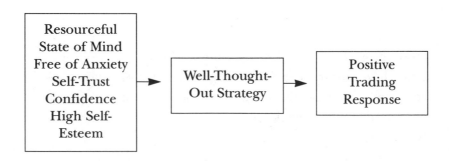

Resourceful State of Mind Free of Anxiety Self-Trust Confidence High Self-Esteem → Well-Thought-Out Strategy → Positive Trading Response

Psychological characteristics of the winning state of mind:
- Expect the best of yourself.
- Establish a personal standard of excellence.
- Create an internal atmosphere for success based on compelling motivation and focus.
- Communicate effectively with yourself; be positive, resourceful, self-empowering.

Positive imagery. We have the power and ability to choose what imagery we process in our minds and bodies. We can literally choose the character and intensity of the images (feeling on a physical level) that are of a visual, auditory, and kinesthetic (physical) nature. We can see failure or success, trading loss or market information, paralyzing circumstances or trading opportunities. It is your mind—you run it!

Visual imagery that enhances performance:
- Picturing success
- Seeing yourself in control
- Looking competent, relaxed, confident, positive
- Viewing a positive visual image that improves your performance

Auditory imagery that enhances performance:
- Hearing the voice of confidence
- The sounds of "I knew I was right"
- The voice of positive expectation

Kinesthetic imagery that enhances trading performance:
- Body feels light, confident.
- Body is energized, strong.
- Focus is direct and alert.
- Breathing is relaxed, effortless, long, and deep.

Internal process for enhancing state:

Visual	*Auditory*	*Kinesthetic*
Brightness	Loudness	Even
Color	Duration	Warm
Contrast	Pitch	Cold
Distance	Tone	Pulsating
Location	Location	Intermittent
Shape	Directions	Strong
Size	Rhythm	Weak

Positive beliefs that enhance state:

- I believe I am or will be a successful trader.
- I believe I can achieve excellent results in my trading.
- I believe I can identify and execute winning trades.
- I believe I can trade with confidence.
- I believe I can trade effortlessly and automatically.
- I believe each day's performance is fresh.
- I believe I am personally responsible for all my trading results.
- I believe I can be successful without being perfect.
- I believe my performance as a trader does not reflect on my self-worth.
- I believe one bad trade is just that.
- I believe trading is a process.
- I believe that by believing in myself and in any proven methodology, and by approaching trading each day with a fresh, positive state of mind, I possess the ultimate trading edge.

Mental conditioning. The psychological skills necessary to trade successfully require ongoing conditioning. They must be practiced day in and day out. They are at least as important as your daily chart work!

IV. Learn the Essential Elements of a Successful Trading Strategy

This list and the discussion that follow encompass what I believe to be the 15 essential elements of a successful trading strategy:

1. Assumes personal responsibility for all market actions
2. Takes into consideration your motivation for trading
3. Allows you to trade to win
4. Establishes goals and formulates a plan to take action
5. Controls anxiety
6. Creates a point of focus
7. Is consistent and congruent with your personality
8. Allows you to have an edge
9. Is automatic-effortless-decisive in its implementation
10. Manages risk and assumes losses
11. Allows for patience and trading in a resourceful state of mind
12. Is profit-oriented—practical as opposed to theoretical
13. Leaves no uncertainty
14. Allows you to produce consistent results
15. Identifies opportunities

1. Assumes personal responsibility for all market actions. It isn't your broker, your brother-in-law, the chairman of the board of the Fed, the fill, the computer, or the unemployment report—it is you!!! It's a simple fact that must be understood in the adoption of any trading strategy: You produce the results. Good or bad, the buck stops here! The Nordstrom Corporation Policy Manual has just one sentence in it. "Use your own best judgment at all times."

2. Takes into consideration your motivation for trading. Your trading strategy must reflect you motive for trading.

If you like the excitement of being in the market, perhaps you should consider not investing in software that takes four trades a year! It is important that your market behavior be consistent with your motive and motivation for trading.

3. Allows you to trade to win. Most traders don't trade to win, they trade not to lose. An effective strategy adopts a proactive market behavior that allows you to play full out; to buy aggressively at your numbers; to catch breakouts; and to enter and exit at your signals. And yes, to win you have to risk loss.

4. Establishes goals and formulates a plan to take action. Your strategy must have long- and short-range goals built into it. What are you trying to accomplish today? This week? This month? This year? In addition, what specific plan can you adopt (right now) to achieve this goal in terms of outcome, performance, and motivation? Yes, there is a lot to think about!

5. Controls anxiety. We have to deal with a variety of anxieties at all times when we are trading. A well-planned strategy minimizes anxiety by addressing the factors that inevitably produce those feelings (e.g., loss, risk-control, market reentry).

6. Creates a point of focus. The problem with most trading strategies is that in the final analysis there is no point of focus. You must know what you're looking for and what you're looking at. You must be able to distinguish the signal from the noise, winning from losing trades, high-probability from low-probability outcomes.

7. Is consistent and congruent with your personality. How many times have we been consulted by traders who have told us their strategy (system) just doesn't "feel right," "look right," or "sound right"? Too many! If your strategy is going to be successful, it literally must feel good.

8. Allows you to have an edge. Unfortunately there is no "edge" sold at the local department store, ready-made, one size fits all. It is just one more paradox of trading that in order to trade successfully you need an edge, but someone else's edge will do you no good. The saying, "one man's sugar is another man's salt" also applies to the idea of edge. You have to find your own and this fact is essential to having a winning strategy!

9. Is automatic-effortless-decisive in its implementation. "He who hesitates is lost."

10. Manages risk and assumes losses. A good trading strategy has the inevitability of loss built into it, so when you lose it is assumed to be inevitable and not unusual. Risk management assumes that no single loss will ever get out of hand. As in baseball, hitting safely three out of 10 times can pay off very handsomely. Your strategy must inform you with certainty when you're wrong.

11. Allows for patience and trading in a resourceful state of mind. Once the trade is made, your strategy must allow you to remain calm, patient, and focused by presenting you with criteria of an objective (they're really all subjective) nature. You must work out, in your own mind, the contingency plans for dealing with a variety of market scenarios. Anything less is gambling!

12. Is profit-oriented—practical as opposed to theoretical. This point may seem obvious, although in reality it's not. Many traders develop strategies to be consistent with a particular ideological or technical bias rather than to make money. The name of the game is performance! Winston Churchill said, "It is a socialist idea that making profits is a vice; I consider the real vice is making losses." This is a point to be remembered in trading as well.

13. Leaves no uncertainty. Think in probabilities, trade in certainties. Your strategy must allow you to know!

14. Allows you to produce consistent results. Your strategy provides the organization and order to allow you to be consistent. The rest is up to you!

15. Identifies opportunities. According to Anthony Robbins (*Unlimited Power*), "The difference between those who succeed and those who fail isn't what they have—it's what they choose to see and do with their resources and their experiences of life." This also applies to trading. Your trading strategy should allow you to open your eyes and see market opportunities—so that you can act!

Now ask yourself the following series of questions:

- Do I really want to become a successful trader? Why?
- Do I possess the internal skills necessary to succeed?
- What really matters most to me?
- Am I willing to pay the price?
- Am I willing to assume personal responsibility for all my actions?
- Am I willing to start where I am?
- Am I willing to think for myself?
- Am I committed to living up to my full potential?

For the samurai, the true Tao of his discipline was to become the most skillful warrior possible, overcoming all internal and external interferences. Thus in the end he himself became a living embodiments of the essence of the true way: "When your spirit is not in the least clouded, when the clouds of bewilderment clear away, there is the true void. By void I mean that which has no beginning and no end. Attaining this principle means not attaining this principle. The way of strategy is the way of nature." (King, *Zen and the Way of the Sword*)

For the trader, the challenge to perfect his art is just as real. To sum up, these are the essential skills that the traders need to master:

- *Patience*—The trader is able to wait for opportunities to materialize in the market based on a well-thought-out game plan.
- *Discipline*—The trader sees the big picture and responds deliberately.
- *Strategy*—The trading plan is well thought out, limiting losses and letting profit run.
- *Expertise*—The trader is well-prepared, and has done the necessary work to ensure a successful result. The trading strategy is well-rehearsed.
- *Motive*—The trader possesses a long-term motive (e.g., intellectual challenge).
- *Goals*—The trader's goals and objectives are clearly defined.
- *Risk control*—The trader has a highly controlled, clearly defined risk/reward ratio.
- *State of mind*—The trader is operating in a positive, resourceful state, with a high level of self-esteem, confidence and focus, in a relaxed right-brain mode.

The Book of Five Rings, written by Miyamoto Musashi in 1643, is one of the most important samurai texts ever written. Its insights were designed for leaders in all professions who were in search of individual mastery and personal excellence. For traders, Musashi's advice is compelling and contemporary:

Think of what is right and true.
Learn to see everything accurately.
Become aware of what is not obvious.
Be careful even in small matters.
Do not do anything useless.

PART THREE

Nature's Way

The Journey Is the Reward

"To take the master's journey, you have to practice diligently, striving to hone your skills, to attain new levels of competence. But while doing so—and this is the inexorable part of the journey—you also have to be willing to spend most of your time on a plateau, to keep practicing even when you seem to be getting nowhere."

—George Leonard, *Mastery*

"Act out the laws of your inner self,
trust the inherent correctness of your
    instincts,
in this way you will meet success."

—Lao-Tzu, *Tao Te Ching*

In *The Intuitive Trader,* I underscored the point that top traders are not top traders as a result of inheriting a special world's greatest trader gene. Winners are not born, they are made. As we have seen, the most compelling force in our development as traders, or for that matter, as human beings, is the thinking that we engage in and the beliefs about ourselves and the environment that we choose to accept as real. If we do not believe in failure, in effect denying its reality, how then can we be defeated? The only "real" limitations on what we can accomplish are those we impose on ourselves. Imagine always operating from a belief system that has these characteristics: Everything we do happens for a reason... to serve us! No matter how negative the experience, within it are the seeds of an equivalent or greater benefit.

There Is No Such Thing as Failure; There Are Only Results

Consider the life history of this individual:

Failed in business at age 21.
Was defeated in a legislative race at age 22.
Failed again in business at age 24.
Overcame the death of his sweetheart at age 26.
Had a nervous breakdown at age 27.
Lost a congressional race at age 34.
Lost a congressional race at age 36.
Lost a senatorial race at age 45.
Failed in an effort to become vice president at age 47.
Lost a senatorial race at age 49.
Elected president of the United States at age 52.

This was Abraham Lincoln. The point is, experience is how we choose to represent an event to ourselves, whether we are running for the presidency or committing ourselves to becoming consistently profitable traders.

Let's now review the operating beliefs that are characteristics of the top traders. I think they clearly reveal what it takes to perform at the highest levels.

- I believe I am or will be a successful trader.
- I believe I can achieve excellent results in my trading.
- I believe I can identify and execute winning trades.
- I believe I can trade with confidence.
- I believe I can trade effortlessly and automatically.
- I believe each day's performance is fresh.
- I believe I am personally responsible for all my trading results.
- I believe I can be successful without being perfect.
- I believe my performance as a trader does not reflect on my self-worth.
- I believe one bad trade is just that.
- I believe trading is a process.
- I believe that by believing in myself and in my proven methodology, and by approaching trading each day with a fresh, positive state of mind, I possess the ultimate trading edge.

"Failure! There is no such word in all the bright lexicon of speech, unless you yourself have written it there. There is no such thing as failure except to those who accept and believe in failure."

—Orison Swett Marden

Take Responsibility for Whatever Happens

In *The New Market Wizards,* Jack Schwager writes the following:

Understand that you are responsible for your own results. Even if you lost on your broker's tips, an advisory service's recommendations, or a bad signal from the system you bought, you are responsible because you made the decision to listen and act. I have never met a successful trader who blamed others for his losses.

Schwager, who interviewed dozens of Wall Street's and Chicago's most successful traders, concluded that, although the methods employed by exceptional traders are extraordinarily diverse—some were pure fundamentalists, other employed only technical analysis, and still others combined both approaches—specific commonalties were abundantly clear. Schwager's observations and recommendations for attaining what he termed *market wizardom,* are the following:

- Be sure that you want to trade. It is common for people who think they want to trade to discover that they really don't.
- Examine your motives for trading.
- Match your trading method to your personality.
- It is absolutely necessary to have an edge.
- The type of method is not important, but having one is critical.
- Developing a method is hard work. Shortcuts rarely lead to trading success.
- Be realistic in your trading goals. As Schwager writes, "Virtually anyone can become a net profitable trader, but only a few have the capability to become super traders. For

this reason, it may be possible to teach trading success, but only up to a point."

- Good trading should be effortless.
- Good money management and risk control are essential.
- Never risk more than one to two percent of your capital on any trade.
- Predetermine your exit point before you get into a trade.
- Cut trading size down sharply during losing periods. If you lose a predetermined amount of your initial capital, stop trading until you regain confidence in your trading.
- You must have a trading plan.
- Be disciplined. In Schwager's words, "Discipline was probably the most frequent word used by the exceptional traders that I interviewed. Often it was mentioned in an almost apologetic tone. I know you've heard this a million times before, but believe me, it's really important!"
- Independence of thought and action is critical. You must be able to make your own trading decisions.
- Be confident. The top traders believe they've won the game before they start.
- Loss is inevitable.
- Trade only when you feel confident and optimistic. If you think of trading or your own performance in negative terms, don't trade!
- The urge to seek advice about a trading position that you're in is a warning sign that you should get out of your position. As Schwager says, "The urge to seek advice betrays a lack of confidence."
- Patience is essential. Waiting for the right setup or high probability trade greatly increases your chance for a successful result. Schwager warns, "Guard particularly against being overeager to trade in order to win back prior loses. Vengeance trading is a sure recipe for failure."

- It is important to learn how to sit with a position. Schwager counsels, "Patience is important not only in waiting for the right trades, but also in staying with trades that are working."
- Develop low-risk trading ideas.
- Vary bet size according to market conditions and volatility.
- Scale in and out of trades. "Most traders sacrifice this flexibility without a second thought because of the innate human desire to be completely right," writes Schwager.
- Consistency is more important than being right.
- Don't worry about looking stupid.
- Sometimes action is more important than prudence. As Schwager notes, "Waiting for a price correction to enter the market may sound prudent, but it is often the wrong thing to do. When your analysis, or gut, tells you to get into a trade at the market instead of waiting for a correction."
- Catching just part of a market move is just fine. The fact that you are not going to capture the entire trend is no reason not to make the trade.
- Maximize gains, not the number of wins.
- Never have loyalty to a position. It is important to act quickly and to show disloyalty to the trade that has proven itself to be wrong. In other words, get out!
- Don't be afraid to take partial profits.
- Hope is a symptom of a losing trade.
- You must be able to make uncomfortable trades. In other words, execute the trade that is right, not the one that feels comfortable.
- Scared money never wins. You won't win if you are trading out of desperation. "If you are risking money you can't afford to lose, all the emotional pitfalls of trading will be magnified," says Schwager.
- Think twice when the market lets you off the hook easily. This often is an indication that your original idea was correct.

- Open-mindedness is a common trait among all the top traders. Schwager quotes one trader who makes the point this way: "The mind is like a parachute; it's only good when it's open."
- If you are looking for excitement, don't trade.
- The calm state of mind of the trader is essential for trading success.
- Top traders know how to identify and eliminate stress in their trading.
- Pay attention to intuition.
- Top traders love to trade. "In talking to the traders interviewed, I had the definite sense that many of them felt that trading was what they were meant to do—in essence, their mission in life," writes Schwager. "Throughout my interviews, I was struck by the exuberance and love the market wizards had for trading." In short, exceptional traders ache to be great.
- The market can be beat.
- There is more to life than trading. Keep trading in perspective.

There Is No Abiding Success in Trading without Commitment

All significant change begins with a strong overriding desire to succeed. Picture the intensity of Michael Jordan, Steffi Graf, or Tiger Woods. Top-performing traders have a commitment to overcome any hardships or setbacks to achieve their goals. Put simply, they are not afraid to step up to the plate and play the game! In *The Mental Game*, sports psychologist James Loehr writes, "Desire was consistently identified as the chief factor leading to competitive success."

Commitment derives from a love of the process and the discipline to always do the next right thing. When I interviewed Pat Arbor, chairman of the Chicago Board of Trade, he had this to say: "What is the essential characteristic required of a successful trader? It all comes down to one thing. Bottom-line, it's discipline. Discipline is the way you handle yourself no matter what else is going on around you. Having it results in success. Lacking discipline and you're a loser."

Jack Sandner, chairman of the Chicago Mercantile Exchange also spoke of the importance of discipline:

> Discipline. I could elaborate on what that means. It means different things to different people, but I think one of the main ingredients is focus. They say traders have a nice life. They come in at 8:30 or whatever, and they're gone at 1:00. You see their expensive cars going down the expressway. What people don't realize is that a lot happens after the bell rings. The other thing people don't realize is between the opening and closing bell, a tremendous energy is expended in focus, if you're any good at what you do. I don't know one trader that's any good that doesn't really focus 1,000 percent every second on what he's doing, and is consumed by it. And the traders that aren't good, they sojourn. They're lazy and they'll make money sometimes, but they'll get caught. I think it takes a tremendous attention span and focus of attention on exactly what you're doing. If you don't do that, then the discipline can't follow. You can't be disciplined unless you focus, because it's too easy to look away and rationalize.

Commitment allows the trader to perform with determination, maintain a consistent performance, and experience a sense of fun, enjoyment, and challenge.

What All Traders Have in Common

All traders, from the novice to the most highly skilled, have these things in common: they lose, get frustrated, at times feel lousy, and experience stress and disappointment. But the top traders, at varying points in their careers, undertook to develop personal internal strategies to overcome these types of setbacks. They taught themselves specific, however varying, methods for getting around potentially disabling psychological bends in the roads. They taught themselves how to become mentally tough and resilient to the subjective demands exerted on themselves and by the market. James Loehr recommends the following regimen for world-class athletes. I believe it is equally suitable for traders:

- *Always play with great intensity.* "Intensity control is a skill that must be practiced," according to Loehr.
- *Use humor to break tension.* Loehr notes that "Humor often brings perspective, fun, and control to what could well have been an impossible situation. The rule of thumb is this: If you can maintain your sense of humor, you're in control."
- *When pressure mounts, get more aggressive.* "The normal response is to become conservative," notes Loehr. "The strategy of waiting for your opponent to make an unforced error is a dead-end

street in the long run.... It's percentage tennis, aggressive tennis; if you lose the match, you've lost it courageously." For traders, the typical response to a losing position is to wait and see rather than to aggressively go with the market. The top traders play to win; they don't play not to lose.

- *Love the battle.*
- *Crises and adversity are the real tests of mental toughness.* The mental edge in sports is really the knowledge that when things get tough you feel emotionally challenged.
- *Project a great image.* If you project an image of confidence, energy, determination, and control—what you show on the outside is the way you will begin to feel on the inside.
- *Leave mistakes behind.* Look ahead and proceed with a positive expectation.
- *Never run out of options.* The goal for the athlete as well as for the trader is never to run out of options. "You're always probing for that weakness that will give you a new foothold, a creative answer to a stubborn problem," says Loehr. For the trader, mastery is the end result of always being engaged with the winner's state of mind. In equation form it looks something like this:

Mastery

Mastery = Samurai psyche + Spirit of jazz

It doesn't hurt also to add these words from the *Tao Te Ching* to round out the picture: "Without expectation, one will always perceive the subtlety; with expectation, one will always perceive the boundary," and "They succeed and do not boast; they succeed and do not make alarms."

The Winner's State of Mind

Expect the Best of Yourself

In my experience, most traders, in a psychological sense, don't trade to win. They trade not to lose! When you trade not to lose, you can never achieve peak performance. In order to derive the best of yourself, you must take defined risk. You must take decisive and automatic action and do everything in your power to win. Expecting the best of yourself at all times will allow you to create and maintain a resourceful psychological state regardless of trading circumstances or conditions. The real test, of course, is not when things are going great for you, but rather, when things get tough, the pressure is high, and the trading seems to be spinning out of control. At these times it is essential to expect the best of yourself based on your commitment, hard work, and discipline. In other words, confidence based on competence will allow you to stay relaxed, focused, concentrated, highly motivated, and most importantly, in control.

Having said that, I'm reminded of a story I once heard about Arthur Rubinstein, the famous pianist. When Rubinstein was in his 90s, he was asked if his hands ever hurt when he played. Rubinstein thought for a moment and then answered, "Only when I hit the wrong notes!" When times are difficult, that is the true test of how successful you are in applying the psychological skills of trading. The literature is ripe with a wealth of psychological studies that report the importance of positive perception on performance. How you perceive yourself will ultimately determine your outcome. Trading constantly presents us with obstacles and opportunities. Expecting the best of yourself is the best means for dealing constructively with both of them.

Establish a Personal Standard of Excellence

Knute Rockne used to say, "Show me a good and gracious loser and I'll show you a failure." Successful trading is all about winning, internal and external. The key to successful trading, as we have seen, is to feel like a winner even though you may be temporarily losing, representing that loss as part of an overall process of confidence and competence.

Establishing a personal standard of excellence is a minimum standard. The top traders have all learned this. They constantly read and study and refine their techniques. They do what is necessary to consistently win. As one top trader put it, "I try to improve my trading by one percent every day. At the end of the year, this is a staggering number."

Understanding your motives and establishing concrete goals will allow you to maintain a consistently high standard of performance. By defining exactly what steps are necessary to secure your goals, you can routinely adopt appropriate actions. As the English author Thomas Huxley observed in *Technical Education*, "The great end of life is not knowledge but action." Adopting a standard of excellence will permit you to achieve your trading goals and experience the success you are capable of attaining. It was the TV producer Grant Tinker who said, "First we will be best, and then we will be first." This philosophy applies as much to trading as it does to getting top television ratings. Hard work and discipline and belief all combine to establish the standard that will guarantee ultimate success.

"The reason a lot of people do not recognize opportunity is because it usually goes

around wearing overalls looking like hard
work."

—Thomas A. Edison

Create an Internal Environment for Success

In order to be successful as a trader, you must create an atmosphere that is pleasant and comfortable, where your trading can
flourish. You must also create a positive psychological dialogue with
yourself based on empowering imagery of a visual, auditory, and
kinesthetic nature. This will result in a high level of self-confidence
and focused concentration. Trading will also be experienced as
effortless, highly enjoyable, and in control.

Formula for creating a successful internal dialogue:
- *Create imagery that respects you,* that makes you feel important.
- *Don't criticize, condemn, or complain.* Complaining and moaning
  won't help.
- *Keep your ego out of trading.* Concentrate on how you can
  develop as a trader—how you can increase your base of
  knowledge and improve your execution strategies.
- *Work to constantly improve.* Work for excellence, not perfection.
  Excellence provides results; perfection produces ulcers.
- *Concentrate on solutions.* Don't reiterate problems. Identify your
  own strengths and weaknesses. Learn from your mistakes.
- *Take personal responsibility for all decisions—not just the good trades.*
- *Invest your time wisely.* Concentrate on what works. It is essen-
  tial that you direct your focus on the practical and not solely
  on the theoretical.

- *And most important, always remember there is a tomorrow.* Don't try to do it all today!

Communicate Effectively with Yourself

When we conduct trading seminars, we always offer the mnemonic TORCH FIRE to represent the essential ingredients in communicating effectively with yourself:

- **T**rust yourself. Follow your instincts; you will be pleasantly surprised.
- **O**pen your mind to possibilities.
- **R**espect yourself by not speaking harshly to yourself. Stay positive.
- **C**hallenge yourself by setting goals that are realistic and will help to build confidence.
- **H**umor is vital. Remember trading is a game; it can be a lot of fun.
- **F**aith—ultimate belief—in yourself and your proven methodology—is imperative.
- **I**nterest is kept honed by constant improvement on your part.
- **R**esults should be your ultimate focus.
- **E**nthusiasm and energy will keep you in the right state of mind. Enjoy yourself.

Communicating effectively with yourself will bring out your ability and allow you to succeed by making the right trading decisions.

"Your mind is a sacred enclosure into which nothing harmful can enter except by your permission."

—Ralph Waldo Emerson

Know Yourself

"The easiest thing to be in the world is you. The most difficult thing to be is what other people want you to be."

—Anonymous

There is a Talmudic expression that states, "to change and to improve are two vastly different things." To improve at trading or anything else, you must begin by knowing yourself, learning those things that motivate your actions. What role do fear, doubt, and worry play in your life? How important is it for you to be successful? The more you understand about yourself, the more effective you will be at trading and everything else. By learning your current trading motives, you can establish goals and a belief system that will ensure success. By directing your focus and by conditioning yourself to have an ongoing positive internal dialogue in terms of your specific beliefs, feelings, and imagery, you can choose how you as an individual internally represent external market phenomena.

"Go as far as you can see, and when you get there, you will see further."

—Anonymous

"Those who identify with the Tao are likewise welcomed by the Tao."

—Lao-Tzu, *Tao Te Ching*

The Top Traders

Consider the psychological perspectives and positive mental focus of these traders.

Bruce Johnson

I think one of the biggest factors is your psychological makeup—you are what you're born as. I was born in Berwyn, Illinois and for me to go out and buy a $2 million house in Northbrook, I mean that isn't me. I think what happens with many traders is that they kind of get used to a lifestyle. Then, they're forced to keep up the lifestyle. I think you have to be comfortable within yourself and not put yourself against the wall. I think it's important you don't get a bunch of obligations heaped on yourself, where you've got to make $20,000 a month to pay a mortgage or some other obligation. It is very important not to burden yourself with psychological pressure. I know this sounds a little simplistic, but you have to kind of take the market and just kind of live with it. Be clear about the market and not think about a bunch of other stuff that clouds your focus and causes mental pressure.

Jeffrey Silverman

I try to get more inner-focused on whether or not the telltale signs of expansiveness are creeping into my thinking—whether or not the people on the opposite side are getting ready to throw in the towel. That's the moment that you've got to absolutely turn around the position and take the money.

Many other people collect these little sayings. Like Charlie McVane said, "When the ducks are quacking, you have to feed them." That's a very interesting saying and if you can imagine the ducks visually and they are screaming and quacking and they're biting you at your pant legs—when everybody's screaming that they've got to have the position that you have on, you've got to think of them as a bunch of ducks that want to be fed. Until you feed the ducks, you haven't make any money. Bruce Johnson put the same thing a different way and he said, "When the circus is in town, you've got to sell peanuts." Now, that puts it in even a better perspective because the circus isn't going to be here forever. When they want the peanuts, you better sell them to them. I guess if you don't feed the ducks, somebody else will feed the ducks and they'll walk away when they're full. I've never seen ducks walk away, buy if you throw enough food at them, I imagine they will walk away too.

Jack Sandner

I think people who have suffered adversity and have overcome adversity many many times are able to become good traders. In my life, I have had a lot of adversity and overcame it. So I have been positively conditioned by doing certain things. I find a way to overcome adversity. So, for me, trading wasn't that difficult of a discipline to learn because trading is full of adversity, and so how do you overcome it? How do you stay with the program and press on? I think when you grow up and have a lot of life experience with adversity and learn ways to overcome it, you are confident that no matter how bad the situation is you tell yourself, "I can survive." I can think of countless times in trading where things were adverse, but if I didn't have the right attitude, I would have crumbled and walked away and never would have been able to come back.

Leo Melamed

It's the biggest challenge you're ever going to have. It's the most interesting challenge around. It's both a vocation and an avocation because it's all-consuming! And the rewards justify the risks.

But there's no nine-to-five to it. It's a 24-hour occupation. You're in tune with the world all of the time. I would say it's a great attraction for someone who has the right psychology and the right personality. And you must have risk capital, so that if you lose, it won't change your lifestyle. If you can succeed, it is a wonderful experience.

I would caution, however, that there's an enormous downside to trading. You may not succeed. It's very difficult. Don't consider yourself a failure if you don't succeed. Because you might succeed in many other walks of life. If you can't succeed in trading, it doesn't mean you can't be successful in other things. The other downside is that if you do succeed, you're going to have a very short life. Absolutely a much shorter life, but I don't mean in physical years. You're still going to live the same amount of years that you would in any other profession you might have chosen. But the time will move much quicker as a trader. Your day, week, month zips by. It's so exciting. It's so interesting that days are shorter, life is shorter. That's unfortunate. You live the same number of years as your friend down the street that worked in the office, but he had a longer life!

Tom Shanks

In 1985 I was short the yen going into a weekend G7 meeting, and the meeting had the effect of weakening the dollar substantially. The consensus that came out of the meeting was that the dollar was too strong. The currencies opened significantly higher on the following Monday and handed me a big loss. I was psychologically shaken by the magnitude of the loss and concerned that I had done something wrong. I immediately reversed the position, because that was what the system said to do. I discussed it with Richard Dennis later, and he assured me that there was nothing wrong with being short given the chart formation. (We Turtles were taught to ignore fundamentals like G7 meetings.) So I remember the pain of having such a move go against me and my electing to follow the system and reverse. One of Richard's favorite maxims was, "Do the hard thing!" Well, that certainly was hard to do, but it was rewarded very well; the currencies continued to move for many weeks after that in my direction. That was a reinforcing experience. Follow the principles, stick with the systems, and you will be rewarded.

Arlene Busch

I focus and I know what I want. I've always known. I have never been one of those people who say, "Oh, I don't know what I want to do with my life or what I want to be." I've known. And I've always known the steps to take and it would take hard work, commitment, and discipline. A lot of people say, "I want to be President of the United States," but they don't know how to go from where they are now to sitting in the White House! I've always known the steps and was willing to pay the price.

You have to be lucky, but then it comes down to your own abilities, you have to know what you're doing, to face the competition and be there to win!

Jerry Letterman

Mr. Letterman is a member of the Index and Options Market of the Chicago Mercantile Exchange. He has been a floor trader, trading his own account for over a decade.

The best moment I ever had in the market was the '87 crash. I made tons of money. It was great. I was on top of the world. I was 27 years old and made an overnight fortune. I went to New York, stayed in the finest hotels, took limos, wined and dined, and bought jewelry. I spent a lot of money and had a great time.

But if I made a million dollars tomorrow, I would not reenact that scene. I'd put the money under lock and key and not spend a single penny of it! I truly know now that I can handle the peaks and the valleys. So I just try and keep things on a stable line. I don't allow myself to get in trouble.

In the old days I'd get on an airplane, go anywhere in the world, eat at the finest restaurants. I don't do that anymore! I'm strictly a family man who loves to hang out with my children. I go to work and make a living and take it one day at a time.

David Lansburgh

Mr. Lansburgh is a member of the International Monetary Market. He is a floor trader specializing in the Swiss franc.

I was a nationally ranked tennis player for ten years. I used to travel all around the country playing in tournaments. I think trading is very much like a game. When people ask me what makes you good at trading, I think it is the same qualities and attributes that you need to be successful at sports. I definitely think that having a history of success in competitive athletics is a huge advantage. Trading is a game. You are competing against other traders and you're competing against yourself.

I just feel like the discipline is to trade the market. I don't let other traders affect what I do. Obviously, if I see certain things happen, I react. But I just stick to my focus and exploit whatever the market gives me. I'm trading against the market, realizing it has to be given respect all the time.

I think the keys to success in trading are discipline, intuition, good instincts, and being aggressive—knowing when you're wrong, to have the discipline to move. You can't have any opinions. I never have an opinion! People always ask me, what do you think? The less I think, the better I'll do. Just focus on the market's action and respond!

Tom Grossman

I think in retrospect, I was fortunate that my father was a good gambler. I learned by watching him that most people don't know how to play. It's the difference between being a player and being a loser. Most people go to the track or to a casino to get some kind of high, to get a mood change. Or they play to make a quick killing, which is the antithesis of what I would consider "good playing." For others it becomes very expensive entertainment! In retrospect, what was fascinating to me then and still is in my current business is just the joy of gaining an edge over everyone else; not focusing on the end result, the money. I think for me that's the key, to get that edge, whether it's reading the racing form better than the others or maybe feeling that because of your understanding of sports, you can dissect the psychological mood of a team, whatever! Knowing when you really have an edge is an art form. When I went to the track with my father, I can tell you that sometimes on a winning bet he would sit through 40 races before he would place a bet. But when he felt like he had one, the joy he had parading around with that advantage in his mind! The time before the race was more elating to him than the actual victory. Clearly, it was gratifying for him when it did work out, but the emotion of having the edge and knowing he waited patiently for the winner to present itself was a huge high. I think focusing on the process instead of the result has been a significant help for me in trading.

Mike Dever

Trading has taught me that I can usually make anything work if I view it objectively, if I approach it properly. Trading is one of the most challenging things in the world. Some of the other things in life are easy compared to trading, in that you have much more control over them. With trading, although from a systems approach you have certain control, there's still an aspect of it that is left to some sort of a chaotic force or random chance, which you can't control. And of course it's really very different from most other businesses or other adventures people take on, you know like learning to fly, racing cars, skiing, things like that. With all that other stuff, you know, the harder you work at it, you're going to get better at it, but that doesn't necessarily apply to trading.

Trading is something that will always be part of me. I think one thing that surprised a lot of people is that when I stopped the discretionary trading, I didn't feel the need to go back to it. I mean discretionary trading really has a unique nature. You really do start to feel like you have a vision of the future or something. There were times when I'd wake up in the morning, and I knew exactly what to do in the market, and everything was just perfect through the day. It just worked! I've had months where it just seemed like day after day after day everything went according to plan. And when you're trading on a discretionary basis, that is great. It's really neat, and I wasn't sure I'd be able to go to a fully systematic method and get that same psychological satisfaction, but I do.

Toby Crabel

The way I've approached trading has been very consistent with the way I approached tennis. (Toby was a three time All-American and professional tennis player.) I've always been very disciplined about my method of gaining knowledge. I was extremely diligent when it came to practice. I practiced almost obsessively. I practiced much more than anybody else that I knew. I wish I had had the focus and the understanding of my own psychology that I have developed in trading as a tennis player. I think I would have been a much stronger competitor. But I also know that as you look back you always kind of think, gee, how much better I could have done with the knowledge and the wisdom that I have now!

Scott A. Foster

I began to apply different things to my trading models that I was developing and to the rules that I was living by as a discretionary trader. I looked for some way to verify them. I knew from studying classical logic that a universal affirmative will imply a particular affirmative, but the inverse relationship is not true. A particular will not imply a universal. And since I could never gather all the data points out there, and I could never gather all the information, how could there be any certainty? This realization ultimately led me in the direction of probability. It was the only way!

So in general I would say my trading evolved from discretionary ideas into a more objective rule system where I'm 99 percent utilizing a systematic approach. But it's not mathematical. I don't use calculus or algorithms or moving averages or anything like that.

I take the approach that to trade the market successfully, you need some type of edge, some advantage that you believe you have over everyone else. There are two different edges that I have tried to exploit in my trading career. One is based on correlations. It's finding markets at an even tandem and you watch them moving in opposite directions, and then key off one by trading the other, say the bonds and the S&P. You're constantly jumping from thing to thing, trying to stay one step ahead of your competition by finding the next correlation or inefficiency in the marketplace.

The other approach that I'm looking to exploit in the marketplace has really nothing to do with a particular market but rather with identifying inefficiency in all freely traded markets, regardless of whether they're futures, options, or equities. As I became a little bit more objective and systematic in my approach, I gravitated toward this approach. Some people are critical of this view. They say, "Well, don't tell me that S&Ps trade like corn." And I'd say, "Well, yeah, they don't, but at the same time, we only have data on the S&Ps during a bull market." I noticed that if we closed down 700, 800, 900 points in the S&Ps, that the next day there is a tremendously high probability that the market is going to take out the previous day's lows. It seemed like there was some bearishness that hung over for the next day, and if the market moved enough, then people had to readjust their portfolios to this new trading level. Instead of day-trading, I began to hold my shorts for a second day, looking for the market to break through the lows.

I wondered to myself, is this just something particular to the S&P market, or is this something that has nothing to do with S&Ps, and has something to do with how people react to all market extremes? So I got the computers out, and I began to ask the computer, let's look at all the data out there. Let's look at corn, soybeans, the cash S&P. Let's look at any freely traded market out there and try to test that idea. We're going back in time to gain an understanding as to whether or not you're exploiting something that is fleeting or something that's really innate to how people react to price data. That's how we develop our trading laws. We do it by coming up with trading ideas that make philosophical sense. We look at the probability and then test it across all the different data points in order to verify its validity.

Robin Mesch

I'm a musician and seriously thought about a career in music before I went to college. I've heard people say that pattern recognition, which is what I use in my chart analysis, is related to the ability to read and interpret musical scores.

Music creates a flow inside of you. Maybe it creates the internal atmosphere for some intuition, which I think plays an important role in my trading.

There are certain qualities in musical phrases and tones and connections inside the melodies, and there's a lot of detective work that takes place. In the same way, I feel like a detective when I'm examining a price chart. I'm looking for connections. I'm looking for clues. A lot of times, I talk to the chart. I have thousands of studies on my charts, pictures and color codes by which I can immediately see and feel what the chart is telling me.

I think I possess a pretty good humor and mellowness about trading. I keep it fairly contained to the trading room. Not only do I have a good sense of humor but a light touch. And I really do believe there is a karma/dharma aspect to trading. I mean, I totally believe that the experience of analyzing the market, coming in to work, coming up with the trade, is what I'm supposed to be doing because it's giving me a lot of pleasure and fulfillment. So I don't worry and I don't take the losses personally!

David Gordon

Mr. Gordon is an independent equities trader residing in Los Angeles, California.

As traders, we can always make money, but as people how and when do we enrich ourselves? This is all I want now: enough money to live happily and to travel and read. All those things that make us happy.

I'm reminded of a quote from Hippocrates: "Life is short, the art long, opportunity fleeting, experience treacherous, judgment difficult."

Solomon Cohen

Trading has taught me different things about myself at different times, according to how the situation has gone. It has taught me that I can be very disciplined, that I don't have to have external constraints imposed on me. It's taught me that I'm very self-reliant.

Often I can put together the jigsaw puzzle, even though some pieces are missing, and will have an insight into a trade that other traders don't perceive. Sometimes I realize I've been arrogant in the way I've done something.

It's interesting how trading teaches us something about ourselves that we don't necessarily want to know but the information is always instructive.

> "In its own way, basketball is a circus. When the tension builds, I'll often call a time-out to slow the game down and plan our next move. The players will be wiped out, anxiously trying to pull themselves together before they have to make their next run. And after they've taken a drink and settled into their chairs, what do they see out on the court? Young women waving pom-poms, children racing around the floor in go-carts. Grown men in gorilla suits trying to slam-dunk a ball from a trampoline.
>
> "That's when you realize that basketball is a game, a journey, a dance—not a fight to the death.
>
> "It's life just as it is."
>
> —Phil Jackson, *Sacred Hoops*

PART FOUR

The Eye of the Trader

The Essential Is Invisible

"The great Tao extends everywhere,
all things depend on its growth,
and it does not deny them....
It clothes and cultivates all things,
and it does not act as a master.
In the end it does not seek greeting
and in that way the great is achieved."

—Lao-Tzu, *Tao Te Ching*

I have been trading now for over 20 years both on and off the trading floor and have certainly learned this: Trading is a messy and unpredictable business. And the more you try to control it, the greater will be your frustration and disappointment. Simply put, trading has a way with you! The key is to experience each moment with a clear mind and open heart, realizing that you're merely a bit actor in a glorious and inscrutable financial human comedy.

When I began trading some 20 years ago, I was regrettably more impressed with myself than were others and mistakenly thought that the activity in which I was engaged was all about external recognition. The concept of internal satisfaction, in retrospect, seemed quite alien to someone who yearned for château-paced living, where each success or failure was added to his personal report card of self-worth.

For me, trading consisted of striving for perfection in every mechanical and technical detail rather than perceiving it as a journey in search of excellence. I viewed trading as another enemy to be conquered, a fire-breathing dragon standing between me and the Loire Valley; it needed to be slain! It took many years, humiliations, and losses in the market before I knew that viewing trading in this way results in frustration, ambiguity, and distraction. It inevitably causes you to expend valuable energy, blame others, feel out of control, and ultimately have a poor sense of self.

As a graduate student in philosophy in the late 1960s and early 1970s, I had the privilege to study Chinese thought with William De Barry at Columbia University, who at the time was recognized as one of the leading Chinese scholars in the world. Each day before he started class, Dr. De Barry would read to us from ancient manuscripts, a passage from the *Confucian Analects* or a verse or two from the *Tao Te Ching* or *I Ching*. The simple wisdom of these readings had an enormous effect on me, and for someone who was classically trained and preparing for an academic career in philosophy, it seemed both exotic and compelling, like some forbidden intellectual apple dripping with seductive but potentially harmful truths.

There are few predetermined destinations in life, and an occasional first step sometimes takes us on a journey of a thousand miles. And so it was with me. I left the magical world of Dr. De Barry's classroom only to find his humble truth offerings years later on the trading floor of the Chicago Mercantile Exchange. I'll spare the details, but even though I was one of the leading market makers on the floor, where I traded limit position size for my own account, over time I made every mistake imaginable. Read all the stupid things you shouldn't do in any trading book and I've been there, done that!

So when I rediscovered the simple Tao truth I had learned in my youth after a particularly long period of drawdown, a few things became very obvious to me:

- Trading provides a strange but in many ways perfect metaphor for understanding life. It contains much of the comedy and drama of life. There is joy, uncertainty, frustration, pain, and struggle. The ultimate challenge is always self-control and self-mastery. Trading involves courage, optimism, the discipline to succeed, and the intuition that the contest is not you against the market, but rather each trader against himself or herself.

- Trading can be thought of as a spiritual journey for which there is no final destination. It is a continuous and transformative process where each day the trader can change and be born anew. By shifting your attitudes and beliefs, you are constantly redefining an unlimited potential, uncorking personal powers that are eager to express themselves.

- In trading, you experience every possible emotion and psychological state, and success is having the courage to risk failure to learn from mistakes in order to be able to "walk on."

- Success in trading is a natural byproduct of commitment and discipline to a process that is founded on excellence, involvement, focus, and fun. As my grandfather used to say, "You don't dance the hora just to get to the other side of the floor." Our victories are the natural outcome of the process. In the words of the *Tao Te Ching*, "The Tao of nature is to serve without spoiling. The Tao of evolved individuals is to act without contending."

- Focusing on the process of trading will allow you to overcome all the self-imposed obstacles and limitations in your trading.

- Trading can become an exciting Rorschach test for gaining self-realization and overcoming inner demons.
- Trading can be enjoyed not only for the inevitable rewards of an excellent process but also for the pleasure it gives. In addition, understanding that performance is more like a roller coaster than an Amtrak train and that discipline and desire allow you to safely ride the ups and downs.

"The great Tao extends everywhere.
All things depend on it for growth,
and it does not deny them."

—Lao-Tzu, *Tao Te Ching*

In essence what I learned in trading after many years of thinking I knew it all and then some, was that there was another way, a simple (not easy), effective way to attain levels of extraordinary performance with a refreshing, fun-loving, and fulfilling view of life. The legendary basketball coach John Wooden said "It's what you learn after you know it all that counts." For me, this change of attitude meant trading in a state of mind where I felt relaxed, focused, and surprisingly more aware. I no longer struggled to make things happen. I found I wasn't fighting against making mistakes; I realized that they were just an inevitable part of the trading process. I truly felt energized and for the first time was able to let go. This was not a passive letting go or giving up; rather it was allowing myself the inner freedom to trade with confidence in order to effectively respond to whatever new surprise the market revealed.

Why Traders Fail

Many traders, even those who have known exceptional success at one time in their careers, ultimately fail because they lack consistency and cannot attain their trading goals. They fail in achieving these goals for the following five reasons:

1. Self-limiting beliefs
2. Unresourceful state
3. Poor focus
4. Ill-defined trading strategy
5. Lack of physical and psychological energy

1. Self-Limiting Beliefs

Self-limiting beliefs are inhibiting beliefs that traders possess about themselves, the market, or both. Examples of such beliefs are:

- "I don't have enough conviction."
- "I'm never quite sure I know what I'm doing."
- "How can I be sure?"
- "I can't trust my judgment."
- "I don't believe in myself."
- "It's impossible to make money in these markets."

2. Unresourceful State

An unresourceful state is when a trader is in a state of mind that is guided by fear, anxiety, and confusion. Traders reported the following:

- "I'm really angry."
- "God, is this frustrating."
- "I'm too stupid."
- "I'm afraid."
- "I'm too small a player."

3. Poor Focus

Poor focus is when trades are made as a result of distracted concentration. You can't zero in on the essentials. Traders report:

- "Those bad fills always get in my way."
- "I'm always thinking about something else at just the wrong time."
- "I'm so distracted by procedures I don't have time to look at what's really important."
- "I can't see the big picture."

4. Ill-Defined Personal Strategy

An ill-defined personal strategy is characterized by trades that are made by the seat of one's pants. In this condition, trading is nothing more than an immediate response to emotion. Traders who have experience this report the following:

- "I don't have a clear plan."
- "I never know when to take profits."
- "My methodology lacks consistency."
- "Sometimes it works and sometimes it doesn't."
- "How do you know when to get out of a market?"

5. Lack of Physical and Psychological Energy

Traders lack physical and psychological energy when their anxiety levels produce tension that results in physical and psychological fatigue. Traders have told me:

- "These markets totally wipe me out."
- "I just don't have enough energy."
- "The market action just drives me nuts."

What Most Traders Want out of Trading

When I interview traders, I always ask them about their current trading goal. Inevitably the answers, whether I am speaking to a novice or seasoned veteran, are remarkably alike. Following are a sample of trader responses:

- To have more control over my emotions when I trade
- To have more confidence when taking losses
- To be consistently profitable
- To develop a system that is consistent with my personality and to readily apply it
- To define my losses and not dwell on them
- To consistently be aware that trading is a process and not just a series of independent trades
- To have a high level of self-esteem when I trade
- To be a disciplined trader

- To focus on opportunities
- To catch breakouts
- To take all my signals
- To have control over my trades
- To establish limited risk and limitless profit potential
- To become a better trader by constantly trying to learn more—about myself
- To operate completely in the here and now

Characteristics of Winning Traders

- Money is a factor but not an essential motivation for trading.
- Trader is well-rounded in his or her personal life.
- Trader is consistent in methodology.
- Trader assumes personal responsibility for all success and failures. (Yes, I know there are no failures.)
- Trader is results-oriented, focused on process.
- Trader possesses flexibility and resilience and is able to let go.
- Trader has a positive attitude, belief system, and state of mind.
- Trader utilizes decisive decision-making.

Characteristics of Losing Traders

- Money is key.
- Trader has a narrow focus in the market and in his or her personal life.
- Trader is inconsistent in approach and methodology.
- Trader refuses to accept responsibility for actions (e.g., blames bad fill, market conditions, etc. instead of himself or herself).
- Trader operates in conflict.

- Trader has a negative attitude.
- Trader is a perfectionist.
- Trading is dictated by emotion.
- Trader is indecisive.
- Trader is stubborn, closed-minded.

Recipe for Trading Success

- Identify market signal (e.g., point, line, area, etc.).
- React automatically with confidence.
- Feel "good" about the trade because it was the right trade to make, not because it was a profit or a loss.

Psychological Barriers

Unfortunately most traders cannot flawlessly execute this recipe because there are specific psychological barriers that need to be overcome in order to have a successful result. In *The Innergame of Trading*, Howard Abell and I identified the following 13 psychological barriers to successful trading:

1. Not defining a loss
2. Not taking a loss or a profit
3. Getting locked into a belief
4. Getting "Boston-strangled"
5. Kamikaze trading
6. Euphoric trading
7. Hesitating at your numbers
8. Not catching a breakout

9. Not focusing on opportunities
10. Being more invested in being right than in making money
11. Not consistently applying your trading system
12. Not having a well-defined money management program
13. Not being in the right state of mind

1. Not Defining a Loss

No one enters a trade assuming it will result in a loss. No one buys expecting the market has topped out; conversely, no one sells expecting the market to rally to new highs. However, this occurs all too often. So upon entering any market, it is important that you have your downside defined, not after you enter a trade but before! If you are afraid to take a loss, don't trade.

2. Not Taking a Loss or a Profit

There is an old trading axiom, "Your first loss is the best loss." It's true. Losing is an integral part of the process. So is the opposite, taking profits. If the market has reached your objective, don't be afraid to ring the register. Many times the market will not give you a second chance.

3. Getting Locked into a Belief

That is exactly what it is—prison. As George Segal succinctly put it, "The market is the boss." Your belief that silver is going to the moon or the dollar is going to hell in a handbasket is irrelevant. The market tells you everything! Listen! Remember what Yogi Berra said, "You can observe a lot by just watching."

4. Getting "Boston-Strangled"

There is an old Henny Youngman joke that was popular in the early 1960s, before the Boston strangler was in police custody. A man is sitting in his living room, reading the evening newspaper, when he hears a knock at the front door. Walking up to the door but not opening it, he asks, "Who is it?"

The psychopath answers, "It's the Boston strangler."

The man walks back into the apartment, passes the living room and into the kitchen, turns to his wife and says, "It's for you, dear!"

My partner and I relate this anecdote at our seminars as an analogy to taking a trade that you have no control over, from someone else. In other words, a tip is like getting Boston-strangled. Don't do it! This is one door you don't want to open!

5. Kamikaze Trading

This means you're trading like you're a kamikaze pilot on his 44th mission. Perhaps you're feeling betrayed, or angry and you need revenge. Snap out of it! You're going to crash-land.

6. Euphoric Trading

This is the opposite of kamikaze trading. You're feeling absolutely invincible, heroic, and untouchable. Look out!

7. Hesitating at Your Numbers

You've done all this work—evaluating daily, weekly, and monthly charts. You've studied Gann, Fibonnaci, Wycoff, and Elliot wave charts. The market comes right down to your number, line, area, but you can't buy it!

8. Not Catching a Breakout

It's like going to the airport and watching planes take off. Wouldn't it be fun just once to be on board and arrive at an exciting destination?

9. Not Focusing on Opportunities

There are so many distractions in the market. How do you keep your focus clear, laser-straight? How do you get beyond all the head fakes?

10. Being More Invested in Being Right Than in Making Money

In almost every trading room throughout the world, there are people who run around announcing to their colleagues that they have the high/low of every move in almost every market. What they don't possess are profits. The name of the game is making money. And yes, it's only a game!

11. Not Consistently Applying Your Trading System

If it's any good, you have to use it consistently. As the saying goes, "If you don't use it, lose it."

12. Not Having a Well-Defined Money Management Program

You have heard this one many times before, "But the trade looked so good, so right." The object of money management is preservation of capital.

13. Not Being in the Right State of Mind

In my experience, over 80 percent of all trading failure is the result of not being in the right state of mind. The right state of mind produces the right results. As Gene Agatstein observed, "You get exactly the results you want. You produce your own success."

Success in Trading

Successful trading then, in essence, comes down to this: overcoming your personal psychological barriers and conditioning yourself to produce feeling of self-trust, high self-esteem, unshakable conviction, and confidence that naturally will lead to good judgment and winning trades based on a proven methodology. But how do you do it? Patience.

In *Flow: The Psychology of Optimal Experience,* Mihaly Csikszentmihalyi writes:

> Many lives are disrupted by tragic accidents and even the most fortunate are subjected to stresses of various kinds. Yet such blows do not necessarily diminish happiness. It is how people respond to stress that determines whether they will profit from misfortune or be miserable.... Subjective experience is not just one of the dimensions of life, it is life itself.

Read that last sentence again, because to know that as your reality as a trader and human being can significantly benefit the quality of your trading and your life! Walt Kelly's cartoon character Pogo expressed the same idea this way: "We have met the enemy, and he is us." Trading is all about controlling psychic energy, creating internal order out of seeming chaos. The relevant point here is that how you internalize your trading experience is more important than any single event that occurs to you in the market.

Reality

As a trader, there is only one reality that is crucial to act on—your own reality, your particular point of focus. You must possess an independent-minded attitude that allows you to identify and respond to your reality and realize that all market actions you take emanate from the realization of this reality. It is my belief that whatever we see in the market at any time is purely subjective in nature and, in fact, our projection, a current reflection of our emotional and physical states. This is not a novel idea—many others, including Mark Douglas, Richard McColl, Charles Faulkner, Bill Williams, Van Tharp, etc., share a similar point of view. The important point here is to know the difference between an effective market reality (one that works) and one that is an autistic fantasy. Also you must trade from the perspective of your reality to the exclusion of all other points of view. Many of us think that when we are watching the market (e.g., bonds, S&Ps, soybeans, etc.) that we are looking at the same thing, sharing in a common experience. Nothing could be further from the truth!

We may be looking at the same markets, but we are not seeing the same things. We are not hearing the same thing and we are not feeling the same thing. Think about anything that you do in "reality." We may all be in the same room and at that moment in time we all may have a totally different reality. Have you ever walked out on the street after not having had a good night's sleep? When that happens, doesn't the world look a little different outside? If you have a toothache, or if you, let's say, lose a boatload of money in the market, things look a little different, don't they? How about when you are in love? Boy, the world really looks good then, doesn't it? The point is, reality is totally based on perspective. So how would that relate to trading? Well, the answer is obvious. You have to understand what your reality is when you are analyzing and trading the market. And you see, as we have learned, our reality of the market depends on what is available to us at any given time. We project our reality. We cannot do otherwise!

Some time ago, this point was dramatically brought home to me. I was on an elevator going up to my office, and the woman standing next to me kept staring at my tie. She turned to me and said, "Oh, what a great tie." She then closely inspected the tie. As she was leaving the elevator she asked, "They are strawberries, aren't they?" I found this interchange most curious because, you see, there were no strawberries, only large, bright red-and-blue polar bears on my tie. I found this very interesting. I imagined this woman purchasing some strawberries, and placing them on her kitchen table, only to be consumed by a polar bear! That would be a bad batch of strawberries! The funny thing is that happens in the market all the time. How many times do people see bears when there are "really" only bulls! Knowing your market reality and consistently applying your proven market strategies by isolating your particular focus consistently while at the same time feeling good—that is to say acting effortlessly and automatically—is the ultimate key to success.

"Many players believe they must do something very special and different on 'big' points. As a consequence, players often break from the pattern and style of play that got them to the big point. Going for too much too early is a strategy breakdown. Going for the low-percentage winner is particularly tempting on the critical points (to get the high-pressure situation over with), but generally spells failure.

"Another common way of breaking down strategywise on big points is to suddenly start pushing the ball back, hoping your opponent will make an error. Shifting to a very conservative, unaggressive style on the big points in order to keep your errors to an absolute minimum will be about as effective as going for too much too soon. The old dictum, never change a winning game, still holds. Whatever you did to get to the big point, continue doing. As a general rule, you will be most successful if you learn to play offensive, high-percentage tennis on critical points. You become the aggressor and work to get your opponent to make a forced error, without making an error yourself. To do this, you must know your own game well. Your general strategy for big points should be worked out well in advance of your match. And breaking down is when you don't follow it."

—James Loehr,
The Mental Game: Winning at Pressure Tennis

"One can enjoy life even when objective circumstances are brutish and nasty. Being in control of the mind means that literally anything that happens can be a source of joy. Feeling a breeze on a hot day, seeing a cloud reflected on the glass façade of a high-rise, working on a business deal, watching a child play with a puppy, drinking a glass of water can all be felt as deeply satisfying experiences that enrich one's life."

Mihaly Csikszentmihalyi,
Flow: The Psychology of Optimal Experience

"You should exercise unrelenting discipline over your thought patterns. Cultivate only productive attitudes.... You are the product of everything you put into your body and mind."

—*I Ching*

"Our duty to the world is to fulfill our individual potential."

—Steven Spender, British poet

The Top Traders

Anthony Saliba

Mr. Saliba is the managing general partner of Saliba Partners. He is a member of the Chicago Stock Exchange, Chicago Board of Trade, and the Chicago Mercantile Exchange.

Technical analysis didn't work for me because, you know it's just so hard to forecast. And then we tried lots of fundamental analysis—which industries look good and that basically means you just become a stock picker. So for a year and a half or two, I actually experimented with a lot of different strategies, and then when I got down to the floor, I also tried a number of different strategies that were popular at the time. Right.

Well, what happened was, I heard about certain strategies other traders were using with good results. And basically, what it boiled down to was the strategy has to have a beginning and an end. The beginning is, you execute a trade. In actuality, you really should make your second trade first, because when you're making the trade, you already know where you're going with it. That is where and how you're going to hedge it. And for me, that's the beginning of the process of building a position. This allows you to get into the market and manage the trade. I mean, you're thinking about money management from the minute you're in, so you hedge! I think what often happens with people who are looking for ways to improve their trading—they're hearing all these voices all around them telling them there is this Holy Grail, just this one way to do it and so money management becomes an afterthought to the whole process.

That's what I call the hobby approach to trading. "Win the Publisher's Clearinghouse Sweepstakes, find the methodology that works for you." Great trading is all about management. It's money management and strategy management.

Keeping in mind that we have a number of different trading entities, depending of course, on which entity you're speaking of, I would say, predominantly, value determines where we enter. When you're required to make a reasonable return on $50 million in capital, it takes quite a bit of daily return. So in this strategy, we are looking for the ability to sell premium without having your butt handed to you if you're wrong. The question we ask ourselves is the ultimate question: Is the volatility the right level to begin to sell? It takes analysis, historical analysis, which, with one political announcement, you throw that away, too. But you start to lean on certain indicators, and you try to fine-tune what you come to depend upon.

For example, during NAFTA (the North American Free Trade Agreement) things really got pumped up, and I don't think any of the guys around us were willing to admit that this was the big chance to sell premium. In actuality it was the best selling opportunity in years, but not a lot of us took more than a small amount of risk to do it. We let a great opportunity get away. So entry again is the art of it that says, okay, look at what your science is telling you and then factor it in with the political and financial news that's currently in the marketplace. But in the whole scheme of the plan as you think about your entry, the question that has to be asked is all about the exit— what are our possibilities with this trade?

In the early 1980s there was a saying that option traders want to pick up the dimes in front of the bulldozers. The dimes are everywhere. They're lying on the ground just waiting to be picked up. There are some traders who look all around them and say well, how could that be? I can't believe it; it's too good to be true! And that, I think is the interesting part. There are other people who look around and say it's not enough for me. I'm not going to bend down unless there's paper money!

Ultimately it's a matter of what you see and how hard you want to work. I believe first and foremost the commitment to work hard is fundamental to being a successful trader and to developing a trading strategy that will work. The reason I say this is obvious: Nothing comes easy, at least it never has for me. And I find that our hard work is usually rewarded. So we're bending down, picking up dimes and nickels and quarters all day long, and we've got to do a lot of bending, but we make it a point to stay in shape to do that! Another friend of mine who is an expert on market timing looks for 12 trades a year, tops—usually eight to ten trades. And he's in there for the trend, and that's where the big CTAs make their money, because they can't move their stuff in and out fast enough, okay? But, for us, our point of view is different. Our horizon is shorter. We see many strategies that will make money, and one is that there are a lot of little bits of change in the market all day long. From where I sit, scalping 12,000 shares of stock for an eighth is just as good as buying a thousand shares and riding it for a point. And, of course, as you know, Everett Dirksen said, "A billion here and a billion there and pretty soon you're talking about real money."

Jeffrey Silverman

It's very interesting; there are attitudes that are part of being an entrepreneur that are natural, that lead you to having intuitive ideas and answers to problems—ways of thinking that don't occur to people that have a law background, for instance, which is based on precedent, or an accounting background, which is based and focused on facts, or even an economics background, which is based on statistics. We are back to my background and orientation as a trader. I'm always forcing myself to ask, "What are the pragmatic issues at work here? What do I see as the major factors coming out of this analysis that are going to drive the whole thing? What are the important variables that will make it all happen?" There is noise to deal with. The statistics themselves are noise. Within each of the statistics, there are random noise elements, but if you know what to look for there is a signal!

What is really boils down to is belief in yourself and belief in the trade that you put on because you've done your analysis. Which also means you're going to ignore the noise, unless the noise reaches such a painful level to your financial being that there's obviously something that you're missing.

I remember I was involved with the start-up of Commodities Corp. some years ago. They raised $2.5 million through Hayden Stone, one of Shearson's predecessors in trading futures. They had a number of academics involved and one was my finance professor at MIT, Paul Cootner, one of the great minds in finance. Another was my economics teacher, the Nobel laureate Paul Samuelson. There were several other Ph.D.s who had written about the nature and character of the markets. A gigantic debate raged within our organization. All the Ph.D.s argued that a system developed by a trader who was on staff at Commodities Corp. at the time couldn't work because it was a very simple moving-average trading system. As I recall the debate, Samuelson was saying that there was no way this could be profitable. It was his opinion that in the long run all these trend-following systems cannot possible work because the markets are efficient. I remember Cootner saying, and by the way he was the editor of the book, *The Random Walk Character of Stock Market Prices,* that futures prices resemble a random walk. However, Cootner was also very pragmatic. He said, "If it works, let's do it. And when it stops working, let's abandon it!"

There are periods of time where the market does in fact trend and other times when it detrends and goes up and down and chops the trend followers apart until they can't stand it any more and forces them to give up their process until the market again proceeds to trend. I don't know that any particular systems can make someone money. Any kind of a system will work, whether it's a purely fundamental system or a very eclectic one such as mine, or a technical system involving charting and computers. They will work. The key point is that all these systems require a degree of discipline, a degree of being in tune with oneself. What is absolutely essential is knowledge of oneself and willingness to stick to whatever the plan is. And thoughtful sleuthing! You can't learn that by buying a trading program or learning someone else's technical strategy.

Becoming a successful trader involves possessing a state of mind where you are open to all sorts of information. You're researching trades in nonobvious places. Who would think that I could come to the conclusion that the yen is no good by driving a rented Thunderbird in Florida? As Peter Lynch would say, the answers are all around us. We see the economy getting stronger and stronger.

This offers all kinds of scenarios and opportunities. Remember the most interesting and profitable opportunities occur when conventional wisdom is set the other way.

If I can make just one point, which I think is essential: What I do is very simple—I am searching out the perfect system. I am searching out truth in supply and demand. You know there is always joy in being uniquely right doing something that looks absolutely absurd and crazy on the surface.

And the rewards justify the risk, because this is where the whole issue of fading the conventional wisdom is. If you're wrong fading the conventional wisdom, you lose a little. If you're right fading the conventional wisdom, you make a lot, an awful lot! You know, the conventional wisdom as Soros and his crowd were beating down the yen, was that the yen was going down. They beat the market from 95 cents to 89, 87 in that area. And then it blew up in their faces. It went back to where they started. The explosive rally happened because they were all there and they were all pushing. The trades that have the good risk/reward ratios are the ones that nobody believes in precisely because they are priced attractively.

In other words, what we are talking about here is a very sensible, very disciplined approach toward contrary opinion investing, where one uses all of one's sense to try to model what is going on in the minds of all the people involved in the market or all those who are utilizing that commodity, that currency, that interest-rate product. Because unless you have internalized something that is different and better than what the other competitors in this game have as their set of tools, you can't make money You must have an edge and bring something special to the table. Something out of the ordinary. And what I will argue is what Peter Lynch will argue and what Warren Buffet will argue. It's that little special sensitivity for the kernels of truth that are out there lying on the ground. They're waiting and all you have to do is pick them up.

Donald Sliter

Mr. Sliter is a member of the Index and Options Market of the Chicago Mercantile Exchange and has been a major market maker in the S&P 500 stock index contract since 1986.

When I'm trading I'm in a zone. You know, other than trading, I have no idea what's going on. I rarely even look up at the exchange clock or boards or anything. All I do is trade every tick. I hand my clerk cards one after another. He's got a stack of cards three inches high and I don't even have names on them. Many times I don't even know what handle we're trading. I certainly don't believe I'm smarter than everybody else by any means. But I do believe that I'm probably the most disciplined trader on the floor for scalping the size that I do. I've really worked at being able to do that. It took a lot of years and a lot of pain to get here....I love trading, you have to understand that. I'm going to be very upset when they start to computerize and it's going to happen. I'll probably retire. I mean they're already going to these hand-held things. I don't know how I'm going to handle that.

I keep telling you it's unconscious, I get in the zone. I swear to God, it's better than sex! It is! After the trade, I look over my trading cards to see how I did. I would do it even if I lost money, because it's just a gas! I'm not a gunslinger. I trade size, but I'm incredibly careful about what I do. I think that if you go in there and put your time in, and exercise rigid discipline every day, you can do it. No matter what the trade is, I always try to finish it off as a winner. If I buy 50 S&P contracts, 150, whatever, even if I'm wrong, on my next trade, I immediately try to make just one or two ticks on a ten-lot. That makes me feel 100 percent better on the trade. I finish the trade off as a winner. I find for me that works well. You go into the next trade feeling good, feeling better.

Leo Melamed

I think not becoming obsessed with my opinion was to me the biggest threat and one that I consistently violated over the years. So, I know that I didn't always adhere to the best principles of successful trading. I would become imbued with a view and sometimes ended up fighting a market or fighting the tape, as they say. That was my most difficult psychological barrier.

The danger is that the difficult period will throw off your rules and logic. You've got to have a set of rules, whether it's instinctive rules or written rules. Every good trader has that set of rules. I've said a good trader is like a Stradivarius violin. You can play beautiful music on it, but if it's out of tune, even a little bit out of tune, the music isn't very good. In order to be that Stradivarius and continue to be successful, to be on your game, so to speak, you have to stay in tune. When you go through a difficult period, you get out of tune. Suddenly, something emotional is interfering with your thinking and that starts a process where suddenly your logic gets distorted.

Yes, you forget your rules. You violate principles that you know are correct. Suddenly, your whole structure of trading comes apart— you're now doing things that you shouldn't be doing. If you think about it, you're reacting to emotions that you normally wouldn't react to. In other words, that Stradivarius is out of tune. That's the experience that every trader has encountered in one fashion or another.

Sometimes you just have to get out of the position. It's not good nursing the position that is causing this distortion in your trading. I've learned that for me, I have to get out. I have to clean the slate. I have to get away from that particular position. Even if it's for only a day or two or three, sometimes a week. But I have to get away. I have to have a mental cleansing of the slate so that I can be in the right state of mind and look at that market fresh the next time.

There is no good trader alive that doesn't do dumb things. In fact, you've got to be able to admit to yourself when you're wrong. You did a dumb thing. You didn't listen to the warning signal. You violated you own rules. These are dumb things that you did and you've got to do smart things. You've got to be honest with yourself.

Patrick Arbor

Mr. Arbor is an independent trader and principal in the trading firm of Shatkin, Arbor, Karlov & Co. He is the chairman of the board of directors of the Chicago Board of Trade.

Intuition. Gut instinct. If you have it, it calls something up inside of you in a New York second, and as a seasoned spreader, you know what to do with it! I tell my son, Michael, who's in the bond and Eurodollar market, that the only nice thing about being older is that we've got a little more experience, a little more of that information stored in us. It's like Mark Twain said about his father. You know, when he was 16 he was amazed at how dumb his father was, but by the time he got to be 20, he was amazed how much his father had learned in four short years.

If you're in this business for years and years, and you've developed good habits and you're honest with yourself, you have instincts. Call it intuition, gut reactions, you learn how to trust yourself! Sometimes when you meet someone for the first time, you like that person right away. There is a natural attraction. And then sometimes after that you start to second-guess yourself. If you stop to think about it, your first impression is usually the right one. It's the same thing in trading decisions. Generally the first thing that comes to your mind, the first reaction you have, to do it or not to do it, is the right one. The more you think about it, the fuzzier the trade gets.

Howard Abell

Mr. Abell was a market maker on the floor of the Chicago Mercantile Exchange and Chicago Board of Trade. He was president of Abell Asset Management Corp., and is currently a principal of Tao Partners, a Commodity Trading Advisor.

Early on in my career when I first came to Chicago, an old-timer at the Chicago Board of Trade said to me the best traders rely solely on their intuition. It is their gift. That is George Segal's gift. In my view, after 25 years of trading, I believe intuition is the sum total of all the stimuli that traders receive in a instant and also the sum total of all their experiences in the market.

Subconsciously, your mind is helping you to make decisions based on all the stimuli that you really can't consciously process. As an example, George Segal, the greatest trader I know, would be able to stay in a position for a very long period of time, weeks and weeks, and then just one day come in and for no apparent or objective reason say, "Sell out."

Oh, he would say he couldn't sleep or just had a funny feeling. And more often than not, he was absolutely correct. Did he catch every high and low? Obviously not. But that is not really the essential point. The essential point is knowing when to get out of a good position as well as a bad one. They haven't yet invented a market indicator that comes close to George's intuition.

Yes, traders truly have to understand exactly how they are reacting both physically and mentally to the marketplace. They have to understand their own feelings and the emotional process that is taking place when they're taking losses or profits or deciding, sometimes in anguish, whether or not to take a trade.

Traders need to look at what makes the successes successful—and very objectively attempt to make themselves operate in the successful mode all the time or as much of the time as possible. It requires a great deal of introspection and looking at yourself and the trading process under a microscope.

Trading is self-discovery. You can tell who you are and what you are by how you trade. The reward of all this self-analysis is the ability to use what we call intuition. Without the work—without the commitment to put in the time and look at how you are internalizing market events—there will be no strong and reliable intuition in the end.

Peter Mulmat

Mr. Mulmat is a third-generation trader at the Chicago Mercantile Exchange specializing in S&Ps and currencies.

To be successful, you have to constantly be willing to reevaluate what you're doing and be innovative in your trading ideas. I think the most successful traders are always retooling their market theories. They are always readjusting their strategies to current conditions and perceptions. I think everyone else is kind of one step behind. You need to be able to first identify what's absolutely relevant right now. It may be different tomorrow. The worst thing you can do is become complacent. You have to be able to challenge yourself. There are always ways to improve on what you're doing and the methodology by which you do it.

This does not only mean looking at new markets to trade and looking at new ways to trade. For currency traders it may mean just trading during the day or taking advantage of options to hedge positions.

I think you have to be willing to innovate and to constantly be committed to look ahead. Of course, the worst thing to do is to grasp onto what people are doing right now and feel that this will make you successful. You must learn to identify and trust your trading intuition.

Be prepared to work very hard. Be prepared to arm yourself with the educational quantitative tools you need to be able to succeed at trading. Remember the people you're competing against. And it is a competition. You're going against the very best! Like any other competition, be it athletic or scholastic, you won't place in the top unless you're willing to prepare yourself.

"When you change your thinking you change your beliefs; when you change your beliefs, you change your expectations; when you change your expectations, you change your attitude; when you change your attitude, you change your behavior; when you change your behavior, you change your performance; when you change your performance, you change your life!"

—Walter D. Staples

PART FIVE

Zen Moments

The Battleground
of the Mind

"The greatest efforts in sports come when the mind is as still as a glass lake."

—Timothy Gallway, *The Inner Game of Tennis*

"Nature's way is simple and easy but men prefer the intricate and artificial."

—Lao-Tzu, *Tao Te Ching*

When Ed Seykota was interviewed by Jack Schwager for *Market Wizards*, he was asked what a losing trader could do to transform himself into a winning trader. Seykota's response was right to the point when he answered, "A losing trader can do little to transform himself into a winning trader. A losing trader is not going to want to transform himself. That's the kind of thing winning traders do."

Successful trading is the result of years of hard work, discipline, practice, and the realization that risk is the vehicle that allows you to achieve a positive outcome. In *The Engine of Reason, the Seat of the Soul: A Philosophical Journey into the Brain,* Paul M. Churchland states the following:

> The human brain, with a volume of roughly a quart, encompasses a space of conceptual and cognitive possibilities that is larger, by one measure at least, than the entire astronomical universe. It has this striking feature because it exploits the combinations of its 100 billion neurons and their 100 trillion synaptic connections with each other. Each cell to cell connection can be strong, or weak, or anything in between....
>
> If we assume, conservatively, that each synaptic connection might have any of ten different strengths, then the total number of weights that the brain might assume is, very roughly, ten raised to the 100 trillionth power. Compare this with the measure of only ten to the 87th cubic meters standardly estimated for the volume of the entire astronomical universe.

We have limitless minds that provide us with limitless opportunities to cultivate our full potential. Success in trading and everything else in life is the result of intensity fueled by commitment and desire to achieve excellence.

It is important for you to remember how much is truly within your control:

- You can control your thinking if you take the time to become aware of the thoughts you are processing and assume responsibility for them.
- You can control your beliefs and the way you imagine yourself.
- You can control the way you conceptualize the world and visualize your place and future in it.
- You can control the goals you set for yourself and the steps you take to achieve them.

- You can control the way you allocate your time and the way you spend your day.
- You can control what is important to you, with whom you associate, and the focus of your attention.
- You can control the environment you learn and live in.
- You can control your response to situations and circumstances, in and out of the markets, that influence your thinking and behavior.
- You can control the intensity, fun, and desire you bring to all your efforts.

To a very real extent you are the captain of your ship and the master of your soul.

"Those who master themselves have strength."

—Lao-Tzu, *Tao Te Ching*

"They do not display themselves;
therefore they are illuminated.
They do not define themselves;
therefore they are distinguished.
They do not make claims;
therefore they are credited.
They do not boast;
therefore they advance."

—Lao-Tzu, *Tao Te Ching*

The jazz musician Sidney Buchet said, "All the technical mastery in the world won't do you any good if you don't have something to say and the ability to lose your ego." In *Zen in the Markets*, Ed Toppel

states that successful trading boils down to the following seven simple rules:

1. Never add to a losing trade.
2. Only add to a winning trade.
3. Let profits run.
4. Cut losses fast.
5. Don't pick tops.
6. Don't pick bottoms.
7. Let the market, not your ego, make the decisions.

It is obvious that what makes trading so difficult is knowing how
to apply these rules consistently and profitably in the market. Toppel
writes:

> There is something within each of us that has a power
> over our minds that prevents our acting according to what
> we have agreed is the proper course of action. That some-
> thing is present in all of us and is very powerful, more pow-
> erful than anything I know....
>
> Those who rid themselves of their egos are rewarded
> greatly. They are the superstars of their fields. In the markets
> rewards come in the form of profits. In the world of art, mas-
> terpieces are the result. In sports the players are all-stars and
> command enormous salaries. Every pursuit has its own man-
> ifestation of victory over the ego.

In *Zen in the Art of Archery*, Eugen Herrigel describes how a student swordsman progresses to the level of master:

> The more he tries to make the brilliance of his sword-
> play dependent on his own reflection.... the more he
> inhibits the free working of the heart.... How does sovereign
> control of technique turn into master swordplay? Only by

the pupil's becoming purposeless and egoless. He must be taught to be detached not only from his opponent but from himself.

This same idea was expressed by Chungliang Al Huang and Jerry Lynch in *Thinking Body, Dancing Mind*:

Egocentricity is a hindrance to performance. The constant need to live up to self-centered illusions creates unnecessary and inhibiting anxiety and tension. The athlete who needs to boast and impress others is usually doing so out of a feeling of deep insecurity and uncertainty and is wasting a lot of energy.

"Bravado when strong hastens decay;
this is contrary to the Tao.
What is contrary to the Tao comes to an early
    end."

—Lao-Tzu, *Tao Te Ching*

"The Tao of nature
is to serve without spoiling.
The Tao of evolved individuals
is to act without contending."

—Lao-Tzu, *Tao Te Ching*

Top trading is the result, once again, of all the effort, desire, and commitment to improve. Creativity of thought and action projects itself naturally and effortlessly—optimistically—from a state of mind that is relaxed, confident, and available.

The Winner's State of Mind

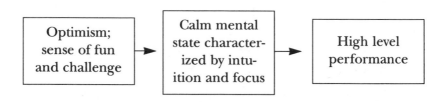

Low-level performance results from state of mind that are anxious, negative, and unavailable.

The Unresourceful State of Mind

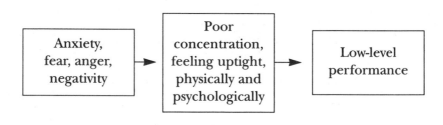

The important point here is that creativity and intuition is the direct result of feeling internally relaxed. In *Flow: The Psychology of Optimal Experience*, Mihaly Csikszentmihalyi interviewed thousands of people to discover the characteristics and qualities of the ideal performance state. He termed this state "flow." It is a unified experience of heightened focus and "flowering" (his term) in the moment where we feel total confidence and control. Flow is characterized by mental calmness, low anxiety, automatic and effortless action, and increased alertness and attention.

Characteristics of Flow

Physical relaxation
Psychological calm
Optimism
Energized demeanor
Active engagement
Fun-loving
Effortlessness
Anxiety-free
Automatic response
Alertness
Confidence
In control
Focus
Ego-free

In *The Inner Athlete, Reaching Your Fullest Potential,* former Olympian Dan Millman describes his discovery of the importance of this relaxed state of mind to his athletic performance:

Beginning with standard psychological theory, I read current studies of motivation, visualization, hypnosis, conditioning, and attitude training. My understanding grew, but only in bits and pieces.... Eventually, I turned to my own intuition and experience for the answers I was looking for. I understand that infants learn at a remarkable pace compared to adults. I watched my little daughter, Holly, at play to see if I could discover what qualities she possessed that most adults lacked. One Sunday morning as I watched her play with the cat on the kitchen floor, my eyes darted from my daughter to the cat and back again, and a vision began to crystallize; an intuitive concept was forming in my mind about the development of talent, not just physical talent but emotional and mental talent as well. I had noticed that Holly's approach to play was as relaxed and mindless as the cat's, and I realized that the essence of talent is not so much the presence of certain qualities but rather the absence of mental, physical, and emotional obstructions as experienced by most adults.

Consider this exchange from an interview that I conducted with Donald Sliter, the largest independent floor trader of the S&P 500 (*The Outer Game of Trading*).

Q: So for you, Don, trading is really like playing basketball. I would like to convey to our readers that even as we're just talking about your trading you are incredibly animated. You are almost jumping out of your seat! You're having such a good time just talking about it! I get the feeling that trading is just a huge high for you.

Don: I'll tell you what; I get in a zone. I'll trade thousands of S&P contracts in a day and I'm just moving in and moving out, feeling great, eating up everything in sight.... I get in the car in the morning and I'm juiced. I can't wait, especially on number days or on expirations. I get so pumped up sometimes. Just the idea that each day is going to be different, that I'm in control of my own situation, my own destiny, every single day. There's nobody to answer to. Everything you do you're either rewarded or you're spanked for.

As you think about the ideal performance state, what is now commonly referred to in sports as "the zone," how does it relate to your own trading?

- Are you relaxed and loose when trading?
- Do you have a sense of inner quiet and calm?
- Do you feel a high level of energy and intensity?
- When you trade are you totally locked into the moment?
- Are you optimistic of your results?
- Are you having fun?
- Is your trading effortless?
- Is your response to market situations automatic?
- Are you totally focused?
- Are you trading with a strong feeling of confidence?
- When you are trading, do you feel in control, no matter what the market reveals?

Achieving Trading Excellence

The eminent sports psychologist James E. Loehr offers a four-step program for achieving athletic excellence in his book, *Mental Toughness Training for Sports: Achieving Athletic Excellence*. It applies equally well to trading.

1. Self-Discipline

This is the stage of commitment. Everything worthwhile begins at this level. Here's where you pay the price: whatever you have to do and whatever sacrifices are necessary to get the job done and reach what you see as your ultimate potential. Yes, it's hard work—it means giving up things you enjoy in order to achieve a higher goal!

2. Self-Control

Loehr describes this stage in the following way: "As you discipline yourself, you experience steady increases in self-control of what you do, what you think, and how you react."

3. Self-Confidence

Self-confidence flows naturally from a commitment to self-control. Self-confidence is an unshakable belief in yourself and your abilities, your proven market techniques, and your ability to execute flawlessly. It comes from knowing, that is believing, that you are in control and are taking full responsibility for whatever happens.

4. Self-Realization

Self-realization is simply living up to your full potential as a human being and as a trader. It is accepting yourself confidently and allowing yourself to think intuitively about the market and everything else. It is in essence opening yourself consistently to all that you are capable of achieving. The famed basketball coach John Wooden described this stage well when he said, "Success is peace of mind, which is a direct result of self-satisfaction in knowing you did your best to become the best that you are capable of becoming."

Mental Conditioning

It is equally important, I believe, for you as a trader to learn how to condition yourself to monitor your thoughts and actions in the market—to listen to what you're saying to yourself and thinking; to develop a tolerance and friendliness, eventually a fascination with your own inner voice; to be mindful of pessimism or negativity and replace the negative talk with something optimistic and constructive. When working with traders I always recommend that they not just try to break bad thoughts or habits—but that they replace them. Here are some examples of energizing thoughts:

Energizing Thoughts

- I always give it my best shot.
- I'm willing to pay any price to achieve my goals.
- I play to win, I don't play "not to lose"!
- I'm going to _____ and have fun while I'm learning.
- I'm in control—of myself.
- I will be successful

One additional point must be made here about the most effective attitude to adopt when making mistakes. If you say to yourself "Mistakes cannot be tolerated" or "I will never make mistakes" or as I've heard traders say over the years, "I'm going to punish myself for making that trade" (usually, in my experience, they end up punishing the people closest to them at that very moment), you are sure to experience frustration, disappointment and anger. It simply is not true that to be a winner you must be perfect. A healthier and more effective attitude is the realization that in order to learn you must make mistakes! Say to yourself, "If I don't make mistakes, I simply won't learn." Develop the confidence in yourself to know that mistakes will be at a minimum when you have created a relaxed internal state.

In *The Mental Game: Winning at Pressure Tennis,* James Loehr makes this point as it relates to tennis. As I have stated, I believe it applies equally well to trading:

If losing is equated with failure, the battle of confidence cannot be won. Your motto should always be, "Win or lose, another step forward." You can find success in a losing effort when you establish clear performance goals prior to the match. You have the potential to learn much more from a loss than a victory. When you set your goals properly, your confidence can continue to grow, independent of your match's outcome.

Characteristics of Creative Thought and Performance

- There is an optimum internal state for each trader.
- Only when the trader feels good (calm, relaxed, etc.) will performance approach optimum levels.
- Consistently high levels of successful trading performance are a direct result of the way one feels physically and psychologically at any moment in time.
- What the trader is processing internally is within his or her control.
- Competitive and sustained trading success is the ability to create internal states of mind regardless of market action.

Zen Moments and Trading

The essential factors, then, leading the traders to an experience of creativity of thought and action are the following:

- A mentally and physically relaxed state of mind
- Confidence
- Optimism
- Focus on the moment
- Energized demeanor
- Elevated awareness and the ability to let go

A tight trading performance is usually the result of one of the following factors:

- Trying too hard, constantly trying to make it happen
- Worrying about past errors and the concomitant fear of repeating those mistakes
- Tentative or unsure execution; straddling the fear of decision, "to trade or not to trade: that is the question"
- Becoming overly concerned with the profit or loss, making the trading decisions cautious, anxious, or mechanical as opposed to effortless
- Obsessed with doing the "right thing"; being conscious rather than unconscious of every move you make in the market; every trade or tactic is a life- and-death struggle, stress-filled and unnatural

Remember the three keys to successful trading:

1. You must feel good to perform great. Your trading performance is a direct reflection of how you feel internally, not the other way around. When you feel good, you perform at high levels.
2. Feeling good is in your control by altering your internal state. Trading performance at the highest levels occurs automatically without conscious deliberation where the right internal climate has been established, based, of course, on a proven method and technical skills.
3. Top trading is the ability to change your emotional state, to move from left-brain dominance to right-brain self-realization, that will guarantee optimum trading performance and will allow you to think and act creatively. The trader must possess the skills necessary to create and maintain positive internal feelings regardless of the market circumstances or situation.

Zen Moments

"Being in the Zone"

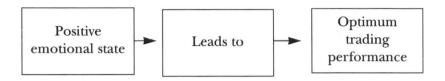

| Positive emotional state | → | Leads to | → | Optimum trading performance |

"The mind then reaches the highest point of alacrity, ready to direct its attention anywhere it is needed—to the left, to the right, to all the directions as required. When your attention is engaged and arrested by striking the sword of the enemy, you lose the first opportunity of making the next move by yourself. You tarry, you think, and while this deliberation goes on, your opponent is ready to strike you down. The thing is not to give him such a chance. You must follow the movement of the sword in the hand of the enemy, leaving your mind free to make its own counter movement without your interfering deliberation."

—Suzuki, *Zen and Japanese Culture,*
on developing a "noninterfering
attitude of mind"

The following description of what it is like to experience the state of mind of "letting go" is based on statements of some of the world's greatest athletes that were complied by Dr. Charles H. Garfield in *Peak Performance: Mental Training Techniques of the World's Greatest Athletes*:

All at once it seems as though everything is working for me. There is no sense of needing to do anything. My actions unfold as they do in pleasant dreams, though my body may be putting out great efforts. I have no thoughts about what I should do or how I should do it. Everything is happening automatically, as though I have tuned myself in on a radio beam that directs my nervous system so that it works in syn-chronization with everything in and around me. I feel insu-lated from all distractions. Time disappears, and even though I know the speed of actions taking place around me, I feel I have all the time I need to respond accurately and well. I am so completely involved in the action that there is not even a question of confidence or the lack of it. There are no issues such as worries about failure or feelings of fatigue. Even feeling momentary fear appears to serve me, changing automatically into a positive force. Success is not an issue, though at the same time it seems natural and easy to achieve. I feel strangely detached from what I am doing even while I am completely in touch with everything, at one with my actions. The whole issue of mind and body separation seems to dissolve, as I feel that both are responding perfectly to my own wishes and inner promptings. I am acutely aware of col-ors, sounds, the presence of people around me, the feeling of being a source of power and energy in this moment in time. It is a trancelike state, but I feel totally in touch with everything around me, with everything within me, as though the usual barriers between me and the outside world have been peeled away, and I am completely at one with myself and the physical world with which I am interacting. It is a wonderful feeling, crisp full of joy, more real than the every day world, going very deep, an experience that rewards me many times over for all the effort I have put in to my sport.

"In spring, hundreds of flowers;
in autumn, a harvest moon;
in summer, a refreshing breeze,
in winter, snow will accompany you.
If useless things do not hang in your mind,
any season is a good season for you."

—Mumon, "The Gateless Gate"

At the crossroads of jazz and samurai consciousness in a cloud cover of inconsistency, complexity, irony, and paradox stands the trader eagerly venturing into the here and now. In a relaxed state of mind, the trader is transformed into an exceptional performer, a juggler of Zen koans with no gurus or experts to help figure out answers. The trader knows the Zen mind is reflected in whatever he or she sees or does in the market. As the masters of old have written, "before enlightenment there is chopping wood and carrying water and after.... there is chopping wood and carrying water!" The trader knows intuitively that creativity and talent thrives from use and withers and dies from neglect, like the lyric from a Billie Holiday ballad, "the strong get stronger and the weak ones fade."

The trader is like a Masai warrior who each day must "face the knife" and hunt the lion with only spear and bare hands. His success will come from relying on his own wits and instincts at the moment of truth, embracing risk as his ally to achieve the desired outcome.

Trading has less to do with the science of computation and more to do with the art of consciousness. It involves invention, imagination, and the courage to just "jump on it." To exploit the hard right edge of a price chart that is in the process of revealing itself for the very first time.

For the trader who is in touch with the Tao, the market is like an open mind: an open window along an open road, a life force to revitalize himself. It teaches the trader about the limitless powers that he or she possesses and the potential to be aligned with its "good vibrations" and rich energy flow.

Trading is a microcosm of life. There is joy, uncertainty, frustration, pain, and struggle. It involves, courage, optimism, humility, and the discipline to succeed. The challenge is ours each day anew. Now greet the market in the spirit of the words of the 18th-century Zen master Hakuin, "So happy to see you. I have nothing to say!"

FOR FURTHER READING

Abell, Howard. *The Day Trader's Advantage.* Chicago: Dearborn Financial Publishing, 1995.

Abrams, J. and C. Zweig, eds. *Meeting the Shadow.* Los Angeles: St. Martin's Press, 1991.

Albert, R. S., ed. *Genius and Eminence.* New York: Oxford University Press, 1983.

Arent, Hanna. *The Human Condition.* Chicago: University of Chicago Press, 1956.

Baer, Jay. *Creativity and Divergent Thinking.* Hillsdale, NJ: Lawrence Erlbaum, 1993.

Barach, Roland. *Mindtraps: Mastering the Inner World of Investing.* Homewood, IL: Dow Jones–Irwin, 1988.

Barron, F. *Creative Person and Creative Process.* New York: Holt, Rinehart & Winston, 1969.

Baruch, Bernard M. *Baruch: My Own Story.* New York: Holt, Rinehart and Winston, 1957.

Benson, Herbert. *Beyond the Relaxation Response.* New York: Times Books, 1984.

———. *The Mind/Body Effect.* New York: Simon and Schuster, 1979.

———. *The Relaxation Response.* New York: William Morrow & Co., 1975.

———. *Your Maximum Mind.* New York: Avon, 1987.

Berne, Eric. The Nature of Intuition. *Psychiatric Quarterly*, 1949, pp. 203-206.

————. *Intuition and Ego States*. New York: Harper and Row, 1977.

Blofeld, John. *The Path to Sudden Attainment*. London Buddhist Society, 1948.

————. *The Zen Teaching of Huang Po*. London: Rider, 1958.

Bronowski, Jacob. *The Origins of Knowledge and Imagination*. New Haven: Yale University Press, 1978.

Butt, Dorcas Susan. *The Psychology of Sport*. New York: Van Nostrand Rheinhold, 1976.

Bynner, Witter. *The Way of Life According to Lao Tzu*. New York: Putnam, 1986.

Cade, C.M., and Coxhead, N. *The Awakened Mind*. New York: Dell, 1979.

Cameron, Julia. *The Artist's Way*. New York: Putnam, 1992.

Cousins, Norman. *The Healing Heart*. New York: Norton, 1983.

Cootner, P., ed. *The Random Walk Character of Stock Market Prices*. Cambridge: MIT Press, 1964.

Csikszentmihalyi, Mihaly. *Creativity: Flow and the Psychology of Discovery and Invention*. New York: Harper Collins, 1996.

————. *Flow: The Psychology of Optimal Experience*. New York: Harper Collins, 1991.

Doboeck, G.J. *Trading on the Edge*. New York: John Wiley and Sons, 1994.

Douglas, Mark. *The Disciplined Trader*. New York: New York Institute of Finance, 1990.

Faulkner, Charles and Freedman, Lucy. *NLP in Action*. Chicago: Nightingale Conant, 1993. Video Tape.

Feng, G and English, J. translators. *Tao Te Ching*. New York: Random House, 1972.

Fisher, Milton. *Intuition*. New York: Dutton, 1981.

Fung, Yu-Lan. *A History of Chinese Philosophy*. Princeton: Desk Bodde, 1953.

————. *The Spirit of Chinese Philosophy*. translator: E. R. Hughes. London: Kegan Paul, 1947.

Galwey, Timothy. *The Inner Game of Tennis.* New York: Random House, 1974.

Garfield, Charles A. *Peak Performance: Mental Training Techinques of the World's Greatest Athletes.* Los Angeles: Jeremy P. Tarcher, 1984.

Herrigel, Eugen. *Zen in the Art of Archery.* New York: Pantheon, 1953.

Huang, Chungliang Al and Jerry Lynch. *Thinking Body, Dancing Mind.* New York: Bantam, 1994.

Jackson, Phil, and Hugh Delehanty. *Sacred Hoops.* New York: Hyperion, 1995.

Jacobson, Edmund. *Anxiety and Tension: A Physiologic Approach.* Philadelpia: J.B. Lippincott, 1964.

Jerome, John. *The Sweet Spot in Time.* New York: Avon, 1982.

Jung, Carl Gustav. *Psychological Types.* Princeton: Princeton University Press, 1971.

Kaltenmark, Max. *Lao Tzu and Taoism.* Stanford University Press, 1968.

King, Winston L. *Zen and the Way of the Sword: Arming the Samurai Psyche.* Oxford: Oxford University Press, 1994.

Koppel, Robert. *Bulls, Bears and Millionaires.* Chicago: Dearborn Financial Publishing, 1997.

———. *How Winning Traders Think.* Chicago: Chicago Mercantile Exchange, 1995.

———. *The Intuitive Trader.* New York: John Wiley and Sons, 1996.

Koppel, Robert, and Abell, Howard. *The Innergame of Trading: Modeling the Psychology of the Top Traders.* New York: McGraw-Hill, 1993.

———. *The Outer Game of Trading: Modeling the Trading Strategies of Today's Market Wizards.* New York: McGraw-Hill, 1994.

Lau, D.C., translator. *Tao Te Ching.* New York, Penguin Books, 1963.

Le Bon, Gustave. *The Crowd: A Study of the Popular Mind.* Atlanta, GA: Cherokee, 1982.

Leonard, George. *Mastery.* New York: Dutton, 1991.

———. *The Ultimate Athlete.* New York: Viking, 1975.

Lin Yutang. *The Wisdom of Lao Tzu.* New York: Modern Library, 1948.

Loehr, James. *The Mental Game: Winning at Pressure Tennis.* New York: Plume, 1990.

————. *Mentally Tough.* New York: Plume, 1986.

————. *Mental Toughness Training for Sports: Achieving Athletic Excellence.* New York: Plume, 1982.

May, Rollo. *The Courage to Create.* New York: Norton, 1975.

McCall, Richard D. *The Way of the Warrior Trader.* New York: McGraw-Hill, 1997.

Merton, Thomas. *The Way of Chaung Tzu.* New York: New Directions, Columbia University Press, 1968.

Mitchell, Stephen, translators. *Tao Te Ching.* New York: Harper and Row, 1989.

Nideffer, Robert M. *The Inner Athlete.* New York: Crowell, 1976.

Oates, Bob. *The Winner's Edge.* New York: Mayflower, 1980.

Pirsig, Robert M. *Zen and the Art of Motorcycle Maintenance.* New York: Morrow, 1974.

Plummer, T. *Forcasting Financial Markets: Technical Analysis and the Dynamics of Price.* New York: John Wiley and Sons, 1991.

————. *The Psychology of Technical Analysis.* Chicago: Probus, 1993.

Poole, Roger. *Toward Deep Subjectivity.* New York: Harper and Row, 1972.

Robbins, Anthony. *Unlimited Power.* New York: Simon and Schuster, 1986.

Schwager, Jack D. *Market Wizards: Interviews with Top Traders.* New York: New York Institute of Finance, 1989.

————. *The New Market Wizards: Conversations with America's Top Traders.* New York: Harper Business, 1992.

Shapiro, Nat, and Nat Hentoff, eds. *Hear Me Talkin' to Ya: The Story of Jazz by the Men Who Made It.* New York: Dover, 1966.

Sperandeo, Victor with Brown T. Sullivan. *Trader Vic—Methods of a Wall Street Master.* New York: John Wiley and Sons, 1991.

Suzuki, D. T. *Zen and Japanese Culture*. Princeton, N.J.: Princeton University Press, 1959.

————. *Zen Buddhism*. Edited by William Barrett. New York: Anchor Book, 1956.

Thomas, Lewis. *The Lives of a Cell*. New York: Bantam, 1975.

Toppel, Edward Allen. *Zen in the Markets: Confessions of a Samurai Trader*. New York: Warner, 1992.

Waley, Arthur. *The Way and Its Power*. London: Allen and Unwin, 1958.

Wallas, Graham. *The Art of Thought*. New York: Harcourt Brace, 1926.

Watts, Alan. *The Joyous Cosmology*. New York: Random House, 1962.

————. *The Spirit of Zen*. New York: Grove Press, 1958.

————. *The Way of Zen*. New York: Randon House, 1957.

Williams, Bill. *Trading Chaos*. New York: John Wiley and Sons, 1995.

Winter, Bud. *Relax and Win*. La Jolla, California: A.S. Barnes and Co., 1981.

Zukav, Gary. *The Dancing Wu Li Masters*. New York: Morrow, 1979.

INDEX

ABOUT THE AUTHOR

Robert Koppel is President of the Innergame Division of Rand Financial Services, Inc., a Chicago-based FCM clearing all major world exchanges. He is the author of *Bulls, Bears, and Millionaires* (Dearborn, 1997) and *The Intuitive Trader* (Wiley, 1996). He is a former long-term member of the Chicago Mercantile Exchange. Mr. Koppel is a principal of Tao Partners. He holds advanced degrees in philosophy and group behavior from Columbia University.

For more information, please contact:

Innergame Division
Rand Financial Services
30 South Wacker Drive, Suite 2200
Chicago, IL 60606
800-726-3088
http://www.innergame.com
e-mail: bob@innergame.com